Living from God's Love

DR SUZANNE PILLANS

Published by Lighthouse Publishing
Grieves Cottage
Drumelzier Haugh Farm
Broughton
Biggar
ML12 6JD

Copyright © 2019

The right of Suzanne Pillans to be identified as the author of this work has been asserted by her in accordance with the Copyright, Designs and Patents Act 1988.

All rights reserved. No part of this publication may be reproduced, stored in a retrieval system, or transmitted in any form or by any means without the prior permission of the publisher. British Library Cataloguing in Publication Data

A catalogue record for this book is available from the British Library

ISBN: 978-1-9108482-2-7

Unless otherwise stated, Scripture quotations are taken from The Authorized (King James) Version. Rights in the Authorized Version in the United Kingdom are vested in the Crown. Reproduced by permission of the Crown's patentee, Cambridge University Press

Scripture references marked NKJV are taken from the New King James Version. Copyright © 1982 by Thomas Nelson, Inc. Used by permission. All rights reserved.

Scripture references marked ESV are taken from The Holy Bible, English Standard Version® (ESV®), copyright © 2001 by Crossway, a publishing ministry of Good News Publishers. All rights reserved. ESV Text Edition: 2016

Scripture references marked NLT are taken from the Holy Bible, New Living Translation, copyright © 1996, 2004, 2007, 2013, 2015 by Tyndale House Foundation. Used by permission of Tyndale House Publishers Inc., Carol Stream, Illinois 60188. All rights reserved.

Cover design by: Esther Kotecha, EK Design
Typeset by Avocet Typeset, Somerton, Somerset, TA11 6RT

FOREWORD

As you take this book in your hands be aware: You are about to undertake an exciting journey with Suzanne Pillans, preacher, missionary and evangelist, as she takes time to share with you from her own heart some of the "secrets of success" in her amazing ministry. This is a journey of faith and discovery.

Written in a simple and easy-to-read style, you will find so many profound truths. With some of them you will find yourself revisiting truths that will hearten and encourage you, reminding you of who God is. Some may be truths opened up in a new and refreshing way; others you will discover for the first time as these principles and issues are made clear, reinforced with real-life examples.

Here you will find no secret formula to protect you from the wiles of the enemy, no silver bullet to the trials and dictates of life. Missing is the panacea to sickness and disease. Rather, you will find a heart of compassion for the lost from a spirit striving to be closer to Jesus while inviting you to take that journey of discovery for yourself, and in the process victoriously deal with all that life, our fellow man, and the devil himself can cast in your path while you are walking in God's love and power.

The truths shared have been learned from personal experience, gained by knowing the Word, a developing relationship with Jesus and a heart of obedience. There are many practical examples, some learned along the way, some discovered in hindsight as Suzanne sometimes looks back at what God did as a result of her walk in Him.

This book is not profound. It is not a tome of deep secrets hard to understand. It is not a theological treatise, nor is it intended to be so.

Rather it is an easy read, uncomplicated, loving. It is a read you will return to from time to time for refreshment, encouragement, and insight, and for the pleasure of reading an uncluttered expression of who God is, His heart for you, and how to connect. It is a book you will share.

I commend this to you in the sure knowledge you will be enriched and blessed as you turn to each new page.

I commend it with this singular caution, dear reader; read this book at your own risk – you may well be changed a little more into His image and likeness.

Rev. Dr Denis Plant, PhD Christian Ed.

INTRODUCTION

What caused the disciples to praise and worship so gloriously while chained in prison that their chains fell off, the gates flew open and the guard and his family were converted that very hour?

What made Stephen praise the Lord while being stoned to death, or thousands of martyrs glorify God while being killed for their faith?

In the Old Testament, what made the three in the furnace survive?

These people had found something so glorious in God that I wanted to know what it was and to pursue this level in Christ for myself.

Yes, we can look around us today and rarely see such faith. Have we lost something so precious in our easy, materialistic society? I believe so, but this can also change.

In this book I dare to pursue the seven different stages in getting to know God, to actually begin to come into this level of faith in Him. Jesus is coming back very soon now and times will get harder first.

I believe that God is looking for people that He can raise up as His forerunners today to walk in a level of faith that will challenge and change many lives.

The goal of reaching this level of walking in Christ may take time, or even years, as it is taking with me, but our discoveries in getting to know God more are so glorious and so rewarding that our efforts made in this direction are nothing compared to what the Lord gives back to us.

So far the Lord has totally transformed my life and given

me a ministry through which He has done more than I could ever think or imagine. But more importantly than that, He has brought my personal life into a joy, in Him, that is so wonderful that I am now learning how to live out of His great love in a new freedom, contentment and renewed energy.

I have learnt that it is not only possible to "enter into His rest", but we are able to live "from His rest" as well (as I will explain in this book).

It is my prayer that *everyone,* whether in ministry or otherwise, can know that there is available to every believer an intimate relationship with God.

SPECIAL THANKS TO

Sonia Stock, who faithfully edited this book.

Rebecca Pillans, my daughter, who designed the front cover. Email rebeccapillans@googlemail.com for any animation or artwork.

Wilfrid Pillans, my husband, who helped with all the computer work and stands with me so faithfully in the ministry the Lord has given us.

And I thank the Lord for His constant guidance, for without the Lord, this book could not have been written.

CONTENTS

1. THE SEVEN LEVELS OF PRAYER 9
2. HOW TO TRULY YIELD TO GOD 17
   (Unconditional Surrender)
3. TO ABIDE OR DWELL IN GOD 25
4. RESULTS OF LIVING IN GOD 33
5. TO HEAR AND OBEY GOD 43
6. LEARNING TO LIVE BY FAITH 49
7. BREAKING THROUGH INNER AFFLICTION 59
8. LIVING FROM GOD IN OUTER AFFLICTION 69
9. LIVING FROM GOD IN THE PRACTICAL 77
10. LIVING FROM GOD'S LOVE 81
    (To Remain and Live from His Love)
11. LIVING FROM GOD'S REST 89

CONCLUSION 93

TESTIMONY TIME 97

CHAPTER ONE

THE SEVEN LEVELS OF PRAYER

What is prayer? To me it's the source of my life. It's my connecting place with the Most High God. It is offering my worship to Him. It is where I discover myself, my function, my enabling and my purpose.

Prayer is also my resting place. The place where I can connect with His peace and meet with His love. Prayer is my eternal home, on this earth and for all eternity.

Learning to live "at home" in Him gives me an inner joy. A joy of knowing Him, even if it is at such a low, basic knowledge of Him. Yet that knowing Him on a personal level grows and grows – and, I have discovered over the years, knowing Him on an intimate level has no limit.

This is also the place to stop and reflect. How am I doing? Am I living for Him to my full potential? What changes need to happen in my life? Where must I cut back in order to make these changes?

This is also the place to hear Him and His instructions that I need to obey. Here is the source of the ministry He has given me and He is in full charge of it. All I need to do is to hear Him and obey Him and He does the rest. This is the only reason the ministry has been so successful. God has done far more than I could ever think or imagine through it. I am so grateful to Him. My only goal ahead is to keep on hearing Him, keep on obeying Him. Then I know that He will bring **His** vision that He has given me to completion.

Just think a moment. We read in the Scriptures that the Lord knew us even before we were an embryo in our mother's womb. Paul the apostle states that it was God Himself who created you! You are His masterpiece!

For we are His workmanship, created in Christ Jesus unto good works, which God hath before ordained that we should walk in them. Ephesians 2:10

You are so precious in God's eyes, but...but...*Is He as precious in your eyes?*

If He is, you will want to know Him more and discover from Him your role on this earth. You have been created by Him for such a time as this. The only time in the history of mankind where you can contribute your special part. If you do not find this special part that God has created you for, that part will be left undone, for no one else can do it. That part has been reserved for you.

In the Old Testament God gave Moses the job of building the Tabernacle in the wilderness. It was built to teach the people how to approach God. He also gave Moses the Ten Commandments to teach people how they must live and to protect them from the consequences of sin. The Ten Commandments were also used to rule countries and nations.

The Lord told me to build a replica of the Tabernacle on our property in England. I obeyed God in building a rather humble attempt, yet a tent that God actually accepted and blessed with His presence. The Lord then proceeded to teach me, from the Scriptures, some very powerful truths which have transformed my life. They have also become the basis of this book.

One of these truths was how to approach God in prayer. To my horror I discovered I hardly even knew the basics of prayer compared to the Israelites of that day. The Lord then showed me that there were actually seven levels of prayer, all of which flowed naturally with our progression "in worship" through the three rooms of the Tabernacle.

The devil hates it when you pray and will do all he can to distract you. Suddenly the phone will ring, someone will knock at the door, your name is called, or the dog or cat will knock something over. We must not let these outside distractions deter us, but make a determined effort to meet with God.

THE OUTER COURT

The "Outer Court" represents sin and the flesh and it is here where worship begins.

1. *REPENTANCE*

Confession of any sin – in thought, word, deed or things left undone. Here we need to fully examine ourselves and ask for His forgiveness for anything we have done wrong, however small it may be. We cannot approach God with sin in our lives, for sin cuts us off from God. However, the sin offering of sheep or goats looks forward to the only sacrifice that could really deliver us from sin and this was brought to reality by Jesus on the cross. We, therefore, must come to Him in repentance and receive His forgiveness.

LET US PRAY:
Lord, I come to you now. Please forgive me for anything I have done wrong in thought, word, deed or things left undone. Thank you for forgiving me. Please teach me to walk in your righteousness. Thank you Lord, Amen.

2. *THANKSGIVING*

We know when the Lord has forgiven us and this fills us

with thanksgiving. Here we need to truly thank the Lord for His forgiveness. We will then be able to proceed to the Golden Room: the area of the soul.

THE GOLDEN ROOM

The Golden Room represents the area of our soul and the next three levels of prayer.

3. *PRAISE*
Enter His courts with thanksgiving. Enter His courts with praise. Praise Him in prayer. Praise Him in song. Praise Him for who He is.

4. *ADORATION*
You will discover that your praise will turn into the next level, adoration, where you simply adore Him, and then adoration leads to worship.

5. *WORSHIP*
Worshipping Him for who He is, King of Kings and Lord of Lords.

The devil can still try and distract you in this area of the soul (mind/will/emotions). I find he will deter you by wandering thoughts or sudden tiredness. You try to concentrate on prayer, but suddenly you have remembered something that you should have done, or something you forgot, like someone's name, etc. Here one can plan to have a notebook ready. Quickly write it down and return to prayer. Tiredness can be solved by standing up and walking up and down to pray, but don't give up. Rather, think about how the Lord feels, and this will give you the determination to carry on.

Think as to the reason why the devil would want to distract

you. He does not want you to get into the spiritual realm to really meet with God. He knows if you really get into the spiritual realm, he can no longer touch you. When you become that close to God, you become too powerful for him and his cause is lost.

Let us spend some time in praise, adoration and worship now. (Levels 3, 4 & 5)

THE HOLY OF HOLIES

After some time of pressing in in worship, you actually enter into the Holy of Holies and experience worship in the Spirit (the area of the Spirit).

There are different ways of entering in. I find that pouring out my love for Him brings me into His presence. Others may find that listening to beautiful worship music will bring them in. Others may find going on a walk in nature will bring them in (where they are totally alone with God). Others may simply prefer to rest in silence, concentrating on Him. There are many ways of coming into His presence and it is up to each individual to discover his/her best way to approach Him.

At this level the 'hard work prayer' is over and you begin to enjoy the Lord's beautiful presence. Here you can rest in Him, allowing His peace to pour into your whole being, and His great love to envelop you. Here your rushed mind quietens down until you hear His still small voice and you enter the next level of worship.

6. *FELLOWSHIP*
Fellowship is the place of bringing your needs to the Lord, or asking His advice on dealing with certain situations. If you are praying for a certain person, or even a group of people or a village, you can ask the Lord to show you the strongholds above that person, people or village. The

Lord will show you the strongholds and how to pray down those strongholds. He will then give you the strategy to reach that person or people with His healing or the Gospel message or both.

I never come to the Lord with a list of requests, but rather with what I am dealing with at the time, even in practical issues like fixing something or designing something. I am always amazed at the good ideas He gives me and they always work out so well. It is here you come into the final level of prayer.

7. REVELATION
Revelation is when the Father speaks. This is so important. I have my prayer journal open and ready to write His instructions down and then underline them. This may be the next step in the ministry He has given me. It is of vital importance that I obey Him exactly as He has told me to. In His way, at His timing. Not less, not more, but just as He has said. As long as I do that, everything will fall into place and the work will be acceptable and accomplished.

Spend time with the Lord and you will yourself experience some of the above. If you have any difficulty hearing God, know that there are different ways of hearing Him. Each of us is different, therefore we hear Him in different ways. I myself may hear God best through His still small voice. But you may hear Him best through pictures or visions or through reading the Bible. Some may hear Him best through writing down what they think He is saying. Others may even hear God through an audible voice.

When you come out of prayer, you know you have met with the living God. He has built you up, He has instructed you, and as you obey God, He Himself will confirm what He has told you to do with His signs and wonders. He will do it. He will do what you cannot do and His work will be accomplished through your life and obedience.

THINK

Why is it so important to enter His presence?
What are the seven levels of prayer?
Why are repentance and thanksgiving so important?
At what level does praying in the Spirit begin?

Time to reflect/prayer

If you want, you can now go back and get that notebook and pen ready, and read this section again. Or set aside a quiet time to practice entering in from levels 1–7 and start your journey "through the Tabernacle" with the Lord.

The Tabernacle Outer Court

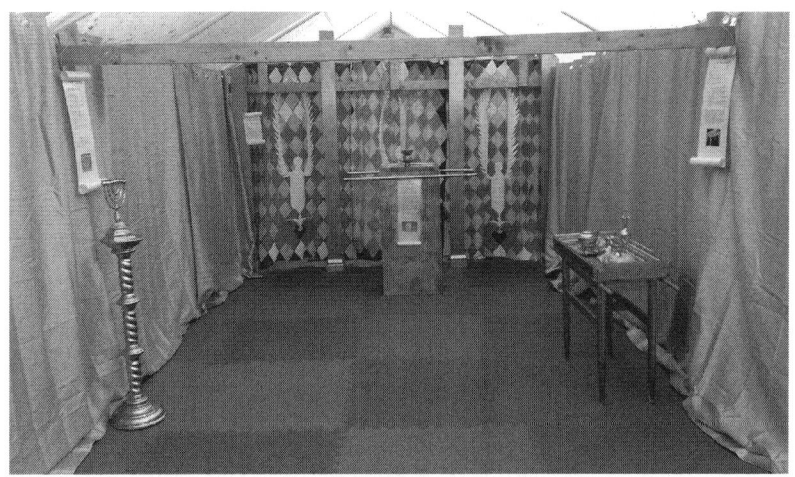

The Golden Room

CHAPTER TWO

HOW TO TRULY YIELD TO GOD

And thou shalt love the Lord thy God with all thy heart, and with all thy soul, and with all thy mind, and with all thy strength: this is the first commandment. Mark 12:30

It means exactly that, and this is the breakthrough – LOVING GOD with every part of your being! The breakthrough into all that He can do in and through your life is rooted in your love for Him and your level of yielding to Him. The difference is so great, so wonderful. He will become first in your life. It will transform everything you do, because this becomes His enabling, His provision, His victory.

But how does one start? How do you love God with all your heart (truly love Him with all your heart)? All your soul (your feelings, desires and affections)? All your strength (all of your pressing in and ability)?

TO LOVE HIM WITH ALL YOUR HEART

This is exactly that! Not just in prayer or talking about it, but loving Him with all our heart should become evident in our lifestyle. It is a lifestyle change – it's about LIVING IT OUT. Living in His righteousness. Having turned from all sin, you have to pursue His righteousness in every area of your life until His gift of righteousness becomes yours.

This was done in the outer court of the Tabernacle that God

gave Moses to build in the wilderness – the area of sin and the flesh. The place where animals were sacrificed for the forgiveness of sin. The place that would point to God sending His only begotten Son, Jesus. Jesus who died in our place, the only true sacrifice that could wash away our sins and give us eternal life.

This is truly serious. **God did that for us – what should our response be?** That of full gratitude, a yielding of all of our heart to Him. To love Him with all our heart and to live out our lives in practical righteousness and truth. This becomes your first offering, your sin offering as our reasonable service, in order to live in righteousness.

TO LOVE HIM WITH ALL YOUR SOUL

This is loving Him with all your soul, as in your will (the decisions you make), your mind and intellect and your emotions. How do you do that? Simply by yielding your soul to Him.

This was done in the Golden Room (Chapter 1) that had the table of showbread, the menorah, which is the seven-branched candlestick, and the table of incense. This area represents the area of your *soul*.

Yielding your will to His will in your life is represented by the table of showbread. And yielding your "will" is a longer process than you might think! It will cause conflict between what you want and what God wants. This is a new concept for some and could even be something scary to do, especially for those who have been used to doing things their way. But be reassured, it is a "process" (a progression) as you yield.

If I could compare it to the illustration of baking bread: first the grain has to be bruised by grinding it very fine. Our will goes through a similar process. It needs to be yielding to God's will, no longer our will. Then, once it is mixed, the bread needs to be moulded. Our will needs to be moulded by God into His will. Sometimes this causes more friction as we still want to go our way, which may be contrary to God's way. We want Him to bless what we do for Him, which may bring about a few good results, but when we instead submit our will to His will, God will do far more than we can ever think or imagine. He has certainly done this in my life and I can never thank Him enough for all He has done.

Then the bread has to be put in the oven. In the same way we also need to be tested. Do I really mean it? Am I really going to obey God when I really don't want to do it, go in that direction, go through the sacrifice or inconvenience that God will expect of me?

Almost everything we do for God will involve a sacrifice or inconvenience in some form or other and the devil will give you many reasons why you should not obey God. This is where so many people give up and fail to press through to what God would really like to bring them into.

But, when we press through in obedience to what God has showed us to do, through the sacrifice, through the inconvenience, GOD'S BLESSING IS ALWAYS AT THE OTHER SIDE, EVERY SINGLE TIME. YOU WILL NEVER REGRET OBEYING HIM; YOU WILL RATHER REJOICE IN HIM.

Then you put the bread on the show table. He lifts you up, that your good works may be seen. But the bread is put in two rows of exactly six, representing discipline. And then incense is put on top of the bread, representing praise, adoration and worship (levels 3, 4 & 5 of the Tabernacle mentioned earlier). Finally, there are two crowns around the table representing "watch" and "pray".

These things will lead us to truly say "Not my will, but your will, my Lord and God."

Take time to reflect

Let us spend some time examining our will, by asking ourselves the following questions:
Lord, have I submitted my will to you, to be refined and moulded into YOUR will for me?
Lord, have I come through your testing of me in a victorious way in You?
Lord, have I walked a disciplined life in you?
Lord, have I truly yielded to you, or am I still fighting for my own way instead?

Time to reflect/prayer

Now let us spend some time in prayer asking the Lord to correct any area; and now, if you feel you are ready, yield (surrender) your "will" to His most precious will.

YIELDING YOUR MIND (THOUGHTS) TO GOD

Yielding your mind/thoughts to Him is represented by the candlestick in the Tabernacle. Now the Lord points us towards our mind and intellect.

Do we only read the passages of Scriptures we like and never the ones we don't like?

Or only obey God in the things that make sense to us and never in the things that don't make sense to us? But the Bible tells us that "*God's ways are higher than our ways, His thoughts higher than ours.*"

But this Scripture does not make it easier for us. Are we going to do what *we* think or what *God* thinks? The choice is ours, of course, but the results will be very different, even life-changing for some of us.

Are we going to chance it, or are we going to submit our thoughts to God?

If we choose to do what we think, we will definitely be chancing it.

If we choose to do what God thinks, His decision will be secure and stable and we will never regret having yielded our thoughts to Him.

We need to yield our full thoughts, mind and intellect to Him and allow Him to renew our minds to think more and more like Jesus. Until we can say "It's not what I think, but what do you think, my Lord and my God?"

Let us examine our thoughts before the Lord

Lord, do I only read the Scriptures I like, and leave the rest?
Lord, have I yielded my thoughts to you? Or do I only think in my own way?
Lord, do I try and think of how you would think on a subject?
Lord, have I fully submitted my thoughts to you, so you can renew me to think more like you?

Take time to reflect/prayer

Let us spend some time in prayer. This could again be difficult for some. But remember, you are yielding out of love. He is your Heavenly Father – everything we do is out of our love for Him.

YIELDING YOUR EMOTIONS TO GOD

Yielding your emotions to Him is represented by the table of incense. We are in control of our emotions. We need balanced emotions yielded up to God, not up and down, good moods, bad moods. We need to discipline our emotions in God and not just function on our own feelings. This too brings a challenge, but if we can harness our emotions, especially in difficult moments, the outcome will be very different and mistakes will be avoided.

Often in worship, our emotions can also be a hindrance. We may have been in prayer for quite a while and not yet entered the Lord's presence. We feel tired or other things are calling for our attention. Yet if we think of how the Lord feels, this will prevent us from giving up, to rather press into Him and enter into the spiritual realm (the Holy of Holies). We will then be able to say "It's not how I feel, but it's all about you, my Lord and my God."

This represents your second offering to God, yielding to Him as a living sacrifice in unconditional surrender.

THINK

Let us examine our emotions before the Lord.
Lord, am I in control of my emotions?
Lord, have I yielded my emotions to you?
Lord, do I think first, before any outburst of emotion?
Lord, have I put how you would feel before how I feel?

Take time to reflect/prayer

Let us examine our emotions before the Lord. You may never have been a calm person, or maybe over the last few years/weeks something has happened in your life and your emotional state is not as it should be. Now is the time to talk to the Lord about it. Yield every emotion to Him.

LOVE THE LORD WITH ALL YOUR STRENGTH (one's own strength and ability)

With all your strength is represented in the spiritual realm by "the Holy of Holies". For me, I see the word "strength" as my determination to press through.

The first veil from the outer court into the Golden Room represented Jesus rising from the dead, but this second veil represents Jesus ascending into Heaven. This is because in the spiritual realm we can ascend into the courtroom of Heaven. There is no longer any limitation in prayer.

This is the beginning of true worship in the Spirit, in *Worship, Fellowship and Revelation (Levels 5, 6 & 7 of Praying Through the Tabernacle, Chapter 1).*

This represents your third sacrifice of worship in the Spirit. The three offerings that we have discussed:

1) The sin offering in the **outer court,** where you confess all your sin.
2) The offering of yourself as a living sacrifice in the yielding of your will, your mind and intellect and emotions in **The Golden Room.**
3) The offering of true worship in the Spirit in the **Holy of Holies.**

These three offerings are acceptable to God and can, on some occasions, cause His presence to come down upon you.

Since I have been teaching on prayer and the offerings we should be bringing to the Lord in this way, I have experienced, along with the people I've been teaching, the glorious presence of God coming down upon us almost every time. People have flocked to the front of the church to kneel and then fall flat on their faces before God in prayer and weeping. Weeping has become the main outcome as people experience the manifest presence of God, some possibly for the first time in years, or even in their lives.

THINK

How should we come to God?
Why is yielding so important?
Why is yielding our emotions important?
What are the three offerings that we can bring to God?

Time to reflect/prayer

A friend of mine has shared how difficult it was for her to "yield" all of herself to the Lord. She realised that this was what the Lord was expecting from her. Due to her great love for the Lord, she prayed, "Lord, I am scared to do this, but I make the decision to yield to you because I love you so much." From that day on her journey of intimacy and dwelling in His presence and listening and obeying His voice has transformed her life.

Take some time over the next few days and seek the Lord to see if there are any areas in your life that the Lord wants. Things you may have had difficulties with. Or – if you feel you are ready – yield yourself to Him now. Our love for Him, and desire to know Him more, will help us to yield to Him.

CHAPTER THREE

TO ABIDE OR TO DWELL IN GOD

He that dwelleth in the secret place of the Most High shall abide under the shadow of the Almighty. Psalms 91:1

The New Living Translation says this: *Those who live in the shelter of the Most High will find rest in the shadow of the Almighty.*

To abide or to dwell? Is there a difference? Or is it just the level of abiding? Also, whose presence are we entering? The Holy Spirit's, Jesus' or the Father's?

Some translations explain it this way: to abide can mean to sit or to tarry. To dwell can mean to have one's abode (to live, to remain, to stay).

To dwell is a level of "abiding". It is likened to a progression, yet there is a difference which we will discuss in this chapter.

Whose presence we enter is also likened to a progression. God is three in one (the Trinity): God the Father, Jesus the Son, and the Holy Spirit.

Initially, some believers may be introduced to God via the Holy Spirit, so therefore will depend on the Holy Spirit at first. However, as their knowledge of the Scriptures increases, they will discover that the Holy Spirit always points us to Jesus. Only to discover that Jesus points us to the Father!

Believers who have had very strict fathers will be more comfortable with Jesus as their main focus (Jesus as their Bridegroom, for example). Yet, those with good father figures will find it easier to approach God (as Father) more quickly.

As God is three in one (Father, Son & Holy Spirit are all God), it is almost as if one moves up the telegraph line of communication from the Holy Spirit to Jesus and from Jesus to Father God, where we come to that place where God truly becomes our loving Heavenly Father.

In the similar way to how Jesus only did what the Father told him, the Holy Spirit only does what He shall hear:

Howbeit when he, the Spirit of truth, is come, he will guide you into all truth: for he shall not speak of himself; but whatsoever he shall hear, that shall he speak: and he will shew you things to come. He shall glorify me: for he shall receive of mine, and shew it unto you. All things that the Father hath are mine: therefore said I, He shall take of mine, and shall shew it unto you. John 16:13-15

How very important it is that we too yield fully to God's will and only do what He tells us to do. As we yield to God fully, then we will also hear Him more fully. We cannot obey Him unless we can hear Him. We cannot hear Him unless we ABIDE in Him in prayer.

In order to enter in, we need to yield ourselves to Him.

TO ABIDE

If ye abide in me, and my words abide in you, ye shall ask what ye will, and it shall be done unto you. Herein is my Father glorified, that ye bear much fruit; so shall ye be my disciples. As the Father hath loved me, so I have loved you: continue ye in my love. If ye keep my

commandments ye shall abide in my love, even as I have kept my Father's commandments, and abide in His love. These things have I spoken unto you, that my joy may remain in you, and that your joy may be full.
John 15:7-11

These are wonderful words on abiding in Him, and then there is yet another wonderful Scripture.

And now, little children, abide in Him; that, when He shall appear, we may have confidence, and not be ashamed before Him at His coming. 1 John 2:28

There are many other Scriptures on "abide", some where the Lord calls us His friends, but when I read these two, I thought that that was it. I was wrong.

When the Lord first encouraged me to learn to abide in Him, I looked up every word on "abide" from Genesis to Revelation, and it took a very long time. I then began to put it into practice and experienced some lovely times in His presence, but always seemed to come out of His presence again.

It was on a plane to Africa that, in prayer, I asked the Lord whether I had learned to "abide" in Him yet. The answer was "no". He said I was more like a watering can: I would come to Him and get filled up and then go back into the world and get empty. Then I would go back to the Lord and get filled up again and then back into the world to get empty again. The Lord told me to enter in and <u>dwell</u> in Him all the time; then I would no longer become empty.

So first I went back to Scripture to look up every word on *"dwell"* from Genesis to Revelation and discovered something truly life-changing. Now in the original Greek, it only speaks on *abide*, and different levels of abiding, but the excellent translation of the old King James Bible cleverly divides *abide* into the first level of abiding, and translates the higher level of "abiding" with the word "dwell". This I found was extremely helpful. Now I could simply look up the higher level of "abiding" with the word "dwell".

I found that in some of the Scriptures on "dwell", the Lord calls us His beloved. I would rather be His beloved than just a friend. These Scriptures really spoke volumes to me.

> *Hereby know we that <u>dwell</u> in Him, and He in us, because He hath given us of His Spirit.* 1 John 4:13

That is straightforward. If we are born again in the Spirit, then it is possible for us to dwell in Him.

> *One thing have I desired of the Lord, that will I seek after; that I may <u>dwell</u> in the house of the Lord all the days of my life, to behold the beauty of the Lord, and to enquire in His temple.* Psalms 27:4-5

All the days of my life? While I am still living on earth?

> Psalms 23:6 then says, *"Surely goodness and mercy shall follow me all the days of my life: and I will <u>dwell</u> in the house of the Lord forever."*

Forever?

> *Blessed are they that <u>dwell</u> in thy house: they will be still praising thee. Selah.* Psalms 84:4-6

Forever? All eternity?

I was beginning to grasp something glorious.

We live in a house on earth, that is our home on earth. We

eat in the house, rest in the house, sleep in the house, do lots of things in the house. Then we go out of the house to go to work, go shopping or many other things. But we always come back to the house again to eat and sleep.

I suddenly realised that in *abiding* I had only been visiting the Lord for a while, to then go back into the world to get empty. **I was getting empty because I was living in the world and not in Him.** Now I was realising that prayer and living in Him was my true home, whilst alive on this earth and for all eternity as well. That meant that living in Him is my only permanent *dwelling* place. My house on earth is only temporary.

Now I was to *dwell* in Him constantly, all the time, and I also came to realise that when I was to go into the world to do the many things that need doing on earth, that the Lord would come *with* me. I no longer became empty because the Lord would come *with* me. This has made a massive difference to the ministry the Lord gave me.

The big question that many ask, though, is *how do you enter into this relationship with the Lord?*

At first it is hard to do. It is as if the Lord is testing us, to see if we are really serious.

One must press in, in exactly the same way as to *abide* in Him. The only difference between *abide* and *dwell* is that *by <u>dwelling</u> you do not come out of His Presence – you stay there.*

To get into His presence is to simply press in; sometimes this can take time. The longest it took me was a day and a half. I was so determined to enter His presence that I was not going to give up until I entered in. When it takes that amount of time to get into His presence, then you definitely do not want to come out again, and that is exactly what the Lord wants.

So you need to press in and press in and press in, with all

your heart, all your soul, all your strength (determination). Press in with love and more love. Then when you come in, do not stop there; press in deeper and deeper until you never want to come out.

As you press in deeper, something amazing happens. It's like you lose your identity. God becomes so big, and yourself so small in comparison, that it's no more me, me, me, but Him. Not what do I want, but what does He want? Not what do I think, but what does He think? Not what do I feel, but how does He feel?

When we come to that level of yielding to Him something glorious happens. It is as if while yielding up into Him, we become infused with His love, His peace, His strength and His presence, where He takes our weaknesses and replaces them with His strengths. Our shyness with His boldness. Our inability with His ability, etc. Until He fully equips us for the work He has for us on earth. He has done this in my life, taking away my fear of going into certain countries, enabling me to go and succeed in the mission He gave me to do there. He will do the same for you as well, in whatever area you need it.

THINK

What is the difference between "abide" and "dwell"?
How do we press in?
What can happen once we press in?

Time to reflect/prayer

Take time to reflect on the difference between Abiding and Dwelling.

Ask the Lord to guide you through this journey to abide in Him. If you sense that you <u>have been</u> "abiding", ask the

Lord to teach you and guide you through to this new level of "dwelling" in Him (dwelling in His presence).

(You may also need to read through the Scriptures on "abiding" and "dwelling" and seek the Lord.)

Then simply press into Him in prayer yourself.

The Holy of Holies

CHAPTER FOUR

THE RESULTS OF LIVING IN GOD

The results of DWELLING (living) in Him are *victory, blessings, everything we will ever need!*

Let's look at some of the blessings we will receive from Scripture.

We will be blessed with <u>all</u> *spiritual* blessings. I am not talking about physical, materialistic things like cars, or earthly possessions, but SPIRITUAL blessings. Blessings that can only come from God. Sometimes the fruit of "living in God" are peace, joy and love. These blessings are given to us through the power of the Holy Spirit.

> *Blessed be the God and Father of our Lord Jesus Christ, who hath blessed us with all <u>spiritual</u> blessings in heavenly places in Christ.* Ephesians 1:3

This means that "all spiritual blessings" that God gives us can affect every area of our lives. We cannot afford to live without these blessings; to do so would be living in spiritual poverty. But Christ takes our poverty and replaces it with His spiritual riches. He takes our curses and replaces them with His blessings. This is part of the divine exchange that He accomplished for us on the cross.

Coming into His presence is one of the ways in which we are able to receive these spiritual blessings.

Let's consider some of these "spiritual" blessings (gifts of grace):

We will become strong in His grace.

Thou therefore, my son, be strong in the grace that is in Christ Jesus. 2 Timothy 2:1

The English Standard Version puts it this way: *"You then, my child, be strengthened by the grace that is in Christ Jesus."*

Here the Lord replaces our weakness with His strength. It is only in His divine grace that this is possible. This divine grace is only possible in Christ Jesus (through the power of the Holy Spirit). It is, therefore, of extreme importance that we take the time in prayer to press in and receive all that we need to live this life on earth as true children of God.

We can receive the wisdom of God (the mind of Christ).

But as it is written, Eye hath not seen, nor ear heard, neither have entered into the heart of man, the things which God hath prepared for them that love him. 1 Corinthians 2:9

The person without the Spirit does not accept the things that come from the Spirit of God but considers them foolishness, and cannot understand them because they are discerned only through the Spirit. The person with the Spirit makes judgments about all things, but such a person is not subject to merely human judgments, for, "Who has known the mind of the Lord so as to instruct him?" But we have the mind of Christ. 1 Corinthians 2:14-16

It is possible for the Holy Spirit to reveal His thoughts to us, His feelings and His purposes as we press in in prayer.

For the Father loveth the Son, and sheweth Him all things that Himself doeth. John 5:20

The English Standard Version explains it this way: *"For the Father loves the Son and shows him all that He Himself is doing. And greater works than these will He show Him, so that you may marvel."*

Through spending much time DWELLING (living) in Him, you will also receive from Him all the understanding you need to then obey Him and achieve all that He wants you to achieve.

<u>We shall receive His anointing</u> (through the power of the Holy Spirit).

But the anointing which ye have received of Him abideth in you. 1 John 2:22

We will then receive His anointing to do His work successfully. We shall become confident in Him.

And this is the confidence that we have toward him, that if we ask anything according to his will he hears us. 1 John 5:14, ESV

Through all that the Lord blesses us with, we have the confidence to do as He has directed us to do. We know that He hears us and will answer us and do it. The Lord has given me confidence in the area of praying for certain sick people whom I know that He wants to heal. Asking according to

His will, when I know He wants to heal them, gives me the faith to pray for them with confidence. Sometimes I will then say to them, "In two minutes you will be able to walk." Within two minutes the miracle then takes place and they are able to stand up and walk. One can never get used to the miracles the Lord does. Each one is so wonderful that one is humbled and full of thanksgiving for what the Lord has done.

We can receive of His love (*Agape* love)

...Nor height, nor depth, nor any other creature, shall be able to separate us from the love of God, which is in Jesus Christ our Lord. Romans 8:39

The love of God is everything we could ever want. God loves us unconditionally; nothing that we do can ever reduce or diminish His love for us. As we spend time with Him, He can reveal this love to us by pouring His love into us and through us to others. We are able to have fresh revelations of His love for us. This brings about our adoration of Him.

We shall live and move in Him.

For in Him we live, and move, and have our being; as certain also of your own poets have said, for we are also his offspring. Acts 17:28

Yes, *"in Him we live and move and have our being"*. Then on earth we, as His children, are also able to live, and move from His being, in His truth and in righteousness. This is truly living from His love.

We shall live in His fulness (abundance).

For it pleased the Father that in Him should all fullness dwell. Colossians 1:19

For in Him dwelleth all the fullness of the Godhead bodily. Colossians 2:9

In Him only can we live in His abundance.

We shall walk in Him.

As ye have therefore received Christ Jesus the Lord, so walk ye in Him. Colossians 2:6

"Walk" here means to live a life conformed to the union entered into with Christ! As His beloved, we can walk "in Him". It's all about yielding, abiding, dwelling in Him.

We are complete in Him.

Rooted and built up in Him, and established in the faith, as ye have been taught, abounding therein with thanksgiving. Colossians 2:7

And ye are <u>complete</u> in Him, which is the head of all principality and power. Colossians 2:10

This "complete" refers to a believer being rooted in Him, because of our intimate relationship with Him! If we live in Him, who is Head of all principality and power, then we will also live in His victory over every evil stronghold, including demons and the devil himself.

The Lord has given us absolutely everything we can ever

need to live a successful Christian life and to serve Him on this earth. If we have truly sought Him with all our heart, entered into His presence and allowed Him to transform our lives, we will be ready *to live from His glorious love* in a powerful way.

What else could we ever need in order to serve Him? We are fully equipped (in Him) for any situation. Yet we have to move out in faith to do what He has asked us to do, in order for His great power to work in and through us. If we stop He stops. If we move out *in obedience*, He moves with us and He does it.

Many say *"But why is the Lord not using me?"* They may have had a prophecy some time ago that God would use them, or they have felt the call, yet nothing has happened.

It is as we move out in faith to minister that we suddenly find that the Lord moves with us. Sometimes I would be called to speak, especially on radio with only a minute's notice. It was only when I opened my mouth to speak that God would put His words in me. These are the times I would speak the best. God has never let me down and He will never let you down either. Step out in faith and see for yourself what God will do.

Living out of His presence in power

> *For though He was crucified through weakness, yet He liveth by the power of God. For we are also weak in Him, but we shall live with Him by the power of God toward you.*
> 2 Corinthians 13:4

If you have any fear of moving out in Him, to do the work *He has asked you to do,* then the above verse is for you. Of course we are weak, but in Him we are strong. It is Jesus who makes the difference within us. It is Jesus who fills us with power (through the Holy Spirit). It is Jesus who enables us, every time, everywhere.

And how does He do it? He does it as we *dwell* in Him **constantly** – the difference is massive. Without Him we are so very weak and what we accomplish is small, but living in Christ, God's power works through us as we are in union with Him.

Living out of His presence in boldness (confidence)

So if the old way, which has been replaced, was glorious, how much more glorious is the new, which remains forever! Since this new way gives us such confidence, we can be very bold. Because of Christ and our faith in him, we can now come boldly and confidently into God's presence. 2 Corinthians 3:11-12

Living (in Christ) in prayer also gives us boldness to go to places where we normally would never consider going, or to do things for Him that you would never believe possible.

One warning! *Only go if you know you have heard God. Going or doing something that you yourself think is good would be moving in presumption only, without Him, and this would be a very dangerous thing to do.*

I myself will always seek the Lord seriously before going, and even ask Him for a confirmation to double check that I have definitely heard God. Once I know for sure that I have heard God, I can then step out in faith and go.

You can become "a well springing up into everlasting life".

But whoever drinketh of the water that I shall give him shall never thirst; but the water that I shall give him shall be in Him a well of water springing up into everlasting life. John 4:14

In the last day, the great day of the feast, Jesus stood and cried, saying, "If any man thirst, let him come unto me, and drink. He that believeth on me, as the Scripture hath said, out of his belly shall flow rivers of living water." John 7:37-38

These two Scriptures say so much, they say it all! Seeking Him, dwelling in Him, drinking from Him (His living waters). This is what will equip you with everything you will ever need, for yourself and eternal life, as well as becoming a river of living water to many people. The Lord will fill you and flow *"His living water"* through your life in His miraculous power.

Everything we receive from the Lord is so positive, you cannot ever receive even one negative thing from the Lord. Negative thoughts and the negatives that follow only come from the kingdom of darkness.

We all have thoughts and our thoughts will influence our brains in a positive way or a negative way. Positive thoughts build up healthy cells in our brain that effect healthy living. Negative thoughts damage and break down our brain cells and could even cause sickness to enter our bodies. Yes, this could even be likened to a virus entering a computer and corrupting all the files, I thought. Good and evil even in a computer? Life is discerning between good and evil.

We are in control of our thoughts. We need to think of any negative thoughts that may be within us, like complaining, jealousy, unforgiveness, criticising others, etc. We need to repent from these negative things and to concentrate on every positive blessing we receive from God instead. By concentrating on the blessings from God, you will enable the fruits of the Spirit to grow in your life and you will be truly blessed.

The blessings mentioned in this chapter are just some of the spiritual blessings we receive from the Lord when we dwell in Him, and these blessings will enable us to live from His love in a very powerful and victorious way. In the next chapters we will go into some of the areas that living in Him will affect our lives.

THINK

List some of the spiritual blessings we receive from living in His presence.
What does He give His blessings for?
How do His blessings change our lives?
What streams of living water are pouring from your life?

Time to reflect/prayer

Ask the Lord to help you to <u>persevere</u> as you grow more in the knowledge and understanding of Him and His great love for you. Remember, this is a journey with the Lord and to get to this point is similar to bearing "fruit" for His Kingdom – fruit takes time to grow! Perseverance is the key.

Suzanne Speaking

CHAPTER FIVE

TO HEAR AND OBEY GOD

We <u>must</u> hear from God.

> *And He said unto them, "Take heed what you hear: with what measure ye mete, it shall be measured to you: and unto you that hear shall more be given."* Mark 4:24

This means the more we give of ourselves to hear Him, the more we will be able to hear Him. He will give us His word and guide us.

> *To Him the porter openeth; and the sheep hear his voice: and He calleth his own sheep by name, and leadeth them out.* John 10:3

As we learn to hear His voice, we will recognise His voice with more and more ease. When we recognise His voice we will respond to Him and follow Him. If we truly hear from God, then we will also know that He will do it. It then becomes a lifestyle of hearing, but it is no use hearing God unless we are also prepared to *obey* Him.

<u>Scriptures on obedience</u>

> *Now therefore, if you will obey my voice indeed, and keep my covenant, then ye shall be a peculiar treasure*

unto me above all people: for all the earth is mine.
Exodus 19:5

This verse says that the Lord values us as His treasured possession when we obey His voice AND keep His covenant. It is important to remember that "hearing" and "obeying" go hand in hand. Obedience to ALL of God's Word, for ALL of what the Bible says we should be doing is essential.

When thou art in tribulation, and all these things are come upon thee, even in the latter days, if thou turn to the Lord thy God, and shalt be obedient unto His voice...
Deuteronomy 4:30

We need to turn to the Lord with all our hearts, and obey Him in all He tells us; then we will be protected, especially in these last days where danger can lurk at a moment's warning.

I would like to share what happened the last time we went to India. It was during the first part of the conference. We were in a large tent speaking to a few thousand pastors and leaders. I had just finished speaking and sat down when I heard the Lord's still small voice say, "Leave this tent now." "Elizabeth," I whispered to my colleague, "the Lord has just told us to leave the tent. Come with me now." I pulled her hand, and we got up together, left the tent and walked into the house behind the tent.

We had only been in the house a couple of minutes when one of the conference leaders walked in. "So glad to see you here and not in the tent. Get up to your room now and lock yourselves in. Twenty gunmen have just arrived in the tent to arrest you. They heard you had come over from England to share the Gospel message." This was because the new president in power had said only the week before, on international television, that anyone who attacked any missionary or evangelist who dared to enter the country would not be held accountable for their actions (in other words they had free rein to take the law into their own hands).

We ran up the stairs to our room on the third floor and locked ourselves in. "Talk about bulletproof obedience," I whispered. "If you wait for the sound of the bullet you are dead, but God has just saved us from that – He told us to leave the tent just in time. We need to thank Him and praise Him for delivering us from those gunmen." We did just that.

The next day, they told us to stay in the room again as the gunmen had returned. It was a little while later that we heard footsteps, and I again heard the still small voice of God. "Don't make a sound." I put my finger over my lips and my other hand to a stop sign. Elizabeth understood. We both kept motionless, hardly breathing as the men knocked loudly at the door and shouted at us to open it. After a while of this the men left.

After this, we could not come out of the room and food was brought to us. I was glad we had a bathroom en-suite. That evening after the gunmen had left, we were called down to preach. The next morning our hosts again spoke through the keyhole: "Don't come out of the room. the activists have come early to catch you." We waited there yet another day and once the gunmen had gone, our hosts came to the door and said, "You can come and preach now, the activists have gone." We then left the room, went into the tent and preached the next message.

The next day was Saturday, but only ten of the activists turned up, this time unarmed. They had been so impacted by the Gospel message they had heard through the other speakers while waiting for us to appear that they wanted to know more about Jesus. Two of them then got baptised that very morning and Elizabeth and I crept to the upstairs balcony, and with our heads covered with colourful head coverings, peeped over the railings to watch them get baptised.

Ye shall walk after the Lord your God, and fear Him, and keep His commandments, and obey His voice, and ye shall serve Him, and cleave unto Him. Deuteronomy 13:4

This Scripture had really become alive for us during that time in India. In fact, all fear had left us. We were so at peace in the Lord's presence and spent hours interceding for the conference.

And Samuel said, "Hath the Lord as great delight in burnt offerings and sacrifices, as in obeying the voice of the Lord? Behold, to obey is better than sacrifice, and to hearken than the fat of rams." 1 Samuel 15:22

When one is overseas doing His work, burnt offerings or sacrifice would be totally useless. It is only obedience that can protect you and get His work done. Nothing else will do, only obedience.

Almost everything we do for the Lord will entail a sacrifice or inconvenience or both. The devil will give you many reasons why you should not obey God, and they will sound reasonable. Possibly this is the reason many give up obeying God at this stage. But I can promise you that if we press on to obey God, through the sacrifice, through the inconvenience, there is always, every time, a blessing on the other side. Never once have I regretted obeying God. On the contrary I have been so glad, so relieved, so thrilled that I obeyed the Lord. It is often when we obey God in inconvenience, sacrifice, or even when it did not make sense, that the miracle happens.

And being made perfect, He became the author of eternal salvation unto all that obey Him. Hebrews 5:9

Jesus was 100% obedient to His Father. He did not do even one thing in His own strength. He only did what the Father showed Him or told Him. Read the Gospel of John and highlight every time Jesus only did the Father's will. If Jesus did only the Father's will, how much should we do only the Father's will? As we obey the Lord, He will do it and our victory comes through Him.

THINK

How will we recognise God's voice and not hear our own voice, or the enemy's voice?
Why is hearing God so important?
What does obedience achieve?
Why is disobedience so deadly?

Time to reflect/prayer

Ask the Lord to open your spiritual ears to hear Him. When you practice hearing from God, He may well give you instructions. It is important to obey what the Lord says. You may make mistakes (many do, no one is perfect), but always check what the Lord is saying against the Word of God.

Removing the Wall

CHAPTER SIX

LEARNING TO LIVE BY FAITH

Out of obedience, we can <u>live by faith</u>.

That the communication of thy faith may become effectual by the acknowledging of every good thing which is in you in Christ Jesus. Philemon 1:6

To me this verse means living out our faith in the practical, that it may become effective. The Lord has definitely tested me in this area, first in the material realm and then in the spiritual realm.

In the material realm, He called us to leave South Africa and come to England, where He would give us a ministry. But it was not that easy. While working for two years for someone else, He told us to sell our place in South Africa. We obeyed, but then we lost three quarters of the price we got, through the rand dropping from two to five rand to the pound almost overnight.

After two years, we were then told that the ministry we thought would be giving us the job were no longer buying the land in Oxfordshire. I cried out to the Lord, "Why are they not buying the land?" "Because you are going to buy it," He replied. "But Lord, we don't have enough money to buy land in England," I stated. "Yes you have," the Lord replied.

We then phoned the ministry up and shared what the Lord had said and they invited us down the following day.

We then managed to buy the land and the Lord restored all that the locust had eaten. On this land, now called "Standlake Equestrian Centre and Ranch", the Lord enabled us to build up a very successful riding school for a living, plus a just-as-successful residential holiday facility for churches and groups of up to fifty people to come and enjoy, plus an international ministry that we run from the profits from the ranch, along with our faithful supporters.

One day during our earlier years, the Lord said, "Now employ someone else to run the riding school; I want you to serve Me." The Lord showed me the person I was to employ, by her asking me for the job. After many years, she is still running the riding school and has been an excellent and faithful employee.

Serving the Lord in the spiritual realm was just as challenging as in the material realm. He sent me to some rather challenging countries and tested my faith to trust Him more and more.

The most challenging was a trip to Nigeria on my own (not to be recommended). The first city we ministered in was Lagos. We then went to minister in Port Hardcourt, and then off the beaten track to a town well inland from the coast.

The pastor put me in a five-storey hotel and I gave him the rest of my money to exchange for me. He never came back that day as he should have done, and I missed the meeting where I was supposed to speak. Nor the second day, nor the third. I would not dare leave the room as I feared for my life. No food to eat, no water to drink, no air conditioning, and the toilet did not flush. Worst of all, I had no phone, no contact with the outside world and of course no money. I looked out of the window to see if I could see a white man at least – any kind of help. None. My only help was from God Himself. I walked up and down that room for three days crying out to the Lord for His help. "Please Lord, don't let that pastor abandon me here, please bring him to change his mind and come back for me."

The hours seemed like eternity those three days, but on the evening of the third day there was a knock on the door. "Who's there?" "Me," came the familiar voice of the pastor. I opened the door in relief. "I thought you had abandoned me," I blurted out. "I did think about it," he replied without thinking.

We then completed the ministry trip together, but it appeared the Lord had taken me to a new level. The miracle healings were outstanding. Five blind people were healed at the same moment; a lady paralysed for twenty-two years could suddenly walk and speak. There were so many healings and deliverances that the people became highly excited and began to shower me with money notes which the ushers gathered up and gave to me.

The money given to me was exactly enough, to the last note, to pay my airfare back to Lagos, so that I could fly home. This is my God. The living God who delivers us from the worst nightmare situations and provides for our every need. There has to be a need in order for the need to be answered. There has to be a sickness for a healing to occur. There has to be a problem for the problem to be solved. Our God does it all and through it teaches us to walk by faith.

Faith is not just for overseas, but also for where you live. When we sold our overseas property, the Lord led us to buy an old shop that had been closed since 1985. Now, what am I to do with a shop? I obeyed the Lord and bought it and began to renovate it. About halfway through I was finding the work difficult and prayed, "Lord, I must have heard you wrong." The Lord replied, "See what I shall do."

Two weeks later I completed the work and heard a knock on the door. As I walked to the door the Lord spoke, saying "See what I have done." I opened the door to see Charlie and

Jacky, both retired, whom I had not seen in years, since the Lord had raised Charlie from a wheelchair.

They told me that God had sent them, so I showed them the shop. "What are we going to do with a shop?" they asked. "Ask God," I replied. They ended up renting the shop.

The Lord then led them into an amazing ministry. They first put Bible verses over beautiful photos and placed them in the shop window. These they changed weekly. and they placed a notice on the shop door saying "Pop in," which then became the name "Poppins".

People from all walks of life have popped into their shop for a coffee and a chat, often to end up receiving Jesus as Lord. They led fifty people to Christ the first year and now lead Discipleship meetings each week as well. We had to take the wall down into the store room last year to enlarge the shop to fit more people into it. Other villages in Wales are now also opening similar shops to bring people to Christ.

And the grace of our Lord was exceedingly abundant with faith and love which is in Christ Jesus. 1 Timothy 1:14

This verse has certainly been realised in our ministry and will be in yours as well.

Hold fast the form of sound words, which thou hast heard of me, in faith and love which is in Christ Jesus. 2 Timothy 1:13

Reading the Bible regularly is so important as you never know when His Word is needed, and we need to know His Word in order to step out in faith on the Word, knowing that behind every word of God is the power of heaven. Whether from the Bible or the *rhema* word – the actual utterance from the mouth of God – obedience is as important.

But without faith it is impossible to please God.

But without faith it is impossible to please Him: for he that cometh to God must believe that He is, and that He is a rewarder of them that diligently seek Him. Hebrews 11:6

Faith comes when we believe and know Jesus is alive. Faith for the impossible is activated through prayer.
Unbelief is the greatest obstacle to overcome.

And Jesus said unto them, "Because of your unbelief: for verily I say unto you, If you have faith as a grain of mustard seed, ye shall say unto this mountain, remove to yonder place; and it shall remove; and nothing shall be impossible for you." Matthew 17:17-20

Faith as small as a mustard seed can move mountains because faith is stronger than mountains: God created the mountains and God cannot lie. That is the ultimate faith God calls us to. To believe that, to walk in it. Not easy.
I was told this story from the book written by Marco Polo; I am not sure if it is in volume one or two, but it's in one of them, and these are not even Christian books. Some Christians had been arrested for their faith in Jesus. The captors had read the Scripture of the mustard seed and said to them, "If your God can move this mountain your lives will be saved; if not we will kill you in three days." The Christians called out to God to move the mountain and on the first day, nothing happened. The second day, nothing happened, and the third day, still nothing was happening. They asked God why nothing was happening and the Lord said that they kept asking Him to move the mountain instead of commanding it themselves to leave in His Name. They then began to pray differently and

took command in the Name of Jesus and to their amazement that mountain suddenly moved through a earthquake and the whole community became Christians.

That by two immutable things, in which it was impossible for God to lie, we might have a strong consolation, who have fled for refuge to lay hold upon the hope set before us. Hebrews 6:18

It is impossible for God to lie. That is so comforting, so reassuring, so faith-building. We can depend on it. In fact, if we look around us at life, this alone makes sense. There is definitely sin, sickness and death. There is definitely a spiritual realm with both demonically negative spirits that plague mankind and the positive Holy Spirit of God that sets us free. These two things alone tell us that Hebrews 6:18 is 100% true.

But the devil is the father of lies. This is easy to believe because one sees it all around us daily. Especially in the area of sin, where people believe the devil and believe his lies and live their lives accordingly. They then come up against the huge consequences of what they have done with deep regret.

Ye are of your father the devil, and the lusts of your father ye will do. He was a murderer from the beginning, and abode not in the truth, because there is no truth in him. When he speaks a lie, he speaketh of his own: for he is a liar, and the father of it. John 8:44

Who is it you believe, God or the devil?

If you believe the devil, the impossible will always stay the impossible for you.

If you believe God and have faith, the impossible will become possible for you.

It's up to you.

In the Scriptures there are varying interpretations of "the Kingdom of God". But let me summarise the kingdoms in this way:

1) The Kingdom of Heaven is run by God and His angels.
2) The kingdom of darkness and hell is run by the devil, the fallen angels and demons.
3) The kingdom of this world is where man is born spiritually dead, unable to understand spiritual things.

But the natural man receiveth not the things of the spirit of God: for they are foolishness unto him: neither can he know them, because they are spiritually discerned.
1 Corinthians 2:14

Through the fall of man in Genesis, when Adam and Eve disobeyed God and listened to the devil by eating of the tree of knowledge and of good and evil, they became spiritually dead, to be born of the flesh only. That is why spiritual things are foolishness to them and they cannot discern spiritual truths.

But we are born again to eternal life into the Kingdom of God in Heaven, where we should be living from right now. That is because we have chosen to receive Jesus as our Lord and Saviour and to pursue and walk in righteousness and truth. This choice enables us to discern spiritual truths. This is because Jesus, through our choice to follow Him, has transferred us out of the kingdom of darkness into His glorious Kingdom of Light (the Kingdom of God in Heaven).

Let's see what the Scripture says:

And Jesus went about all Galilee, teaching in their synagogues, and preaching the Gospel of the Kingdom, and healing all manner of sickness and all manner of disease among the people. Matthew 4:23

We see here how Jesus shows us the Kingdom of Heaven, by the sharing of the Gospel of the Kingdom with the healing of sickness and disease. Healing is part of God's Kingdom.

For the Kingdom of God is not in word, but in power.
1 Corinthians 4:20

Here we learn that the Kingdom of God is not just in word, but in power. The Kingdom of God is real; it works in our everyday lives, especially when we share the Gospel message. Sharing the Gospel message seems to draw the healing miracles of God down upon man in power and reality, as people get healed and realise that God has just healed them.

Now when He was asked by the Pharisees when the Kingdom of God would come, He answered and said, "The Kingdom of God does not come with observation; nor will they say, 'See here!' or 'See there!' For indeed, the Kingdom of God is within you." Luke 17:20-21

Jesus was trying to tell the Pharisees that they needed to receive the Kingdom of God within them. As one either receives evil within, or goodness within, so with the kingdoms. Whatever kingdom we receive is the kingdom we belong to and where we will spend eternity.

This alone makes us realise the importance of receiving and following Christ. He will then transfer us totally out of the kingdom of darkness into His everlasting Kingdom of God in Heaven. We need to receive His Kingdom into our hearts and lives now, so that His Kingdom will truly be within us.

THINK

What is faith?
Why is unbelief the most difficult to overcome?
Name the three kingdoms that I have summarised.
How can we be transferred into the Kingdom of God?

Time to reflect/prayer

If you struggle in the area of faith, spend time with the Lord and ask Him to give you a revelation of <u>His</u> faith. Remember that when you received Christ, you were given a measure of His faith. It is already in you (Romans 12:3).

Worship at Standlake

CHAPTER SEVEN

BREAKING THROUGH INNER AFFLICTION

How many of us battle with limitations from the past?
How do we throw them off?
Will we ever be able to walk free from them?

These questions are asked by thousands of people, but there is a glorious answer and the answer is closer than we expect.

Most of us have limitations of some kind, even if it is only a fear or a rejection of some sort. But others can be dealing with far greater limitations that hinder them badly in their walk of life.

Where do these limitations come from?
They come into our lives through negative experiences from our past. Things our previous generations may have been involved with (e.g. generational curses, soul ties) or even things like lies spoken against us. All such things can build up inside us as strongholds.

How do they enter into our lives?
One way is through the trauma of that negative moment.

How do we deal with them? Can they even be dealt with? Or are they just part of us?

These questions are asked by many. I would like to share how the Lord taught me to deal with them.

"Lord!" I asked, "How am I to write on this?" "How do you get victory over pain, inner conflict, inner bondage or suffering?"

"It is love and love alone," I seemed to hear Him say.

I was walking in the mountains when suddenly the Lord said *"Stop."* I stopped. *"What do you hear?"* He asked. "Water," I replied, "rivers." *"How many rivers?"* He asked. I listened. "At least four, one from each direction," I answered, a little startled.

The Lord continued. *"These are my natural rivers bringing life to wherever they flow. But the rivers of living water that should be flowing through my people are often blocked up by the worries, problems and past hurts of this world. I wish to use you to help unblock some of these past hurts in my people, so that my rivers may flow through them as they should."*

"Lord, how do I do that? Where do I start?" The Lord replied, *"Start in the same way I started with you."*

My thoughts went back to the time I spent in Israel. I'd had the chance to visit Antipatris, where Paul the apostle was kept prisoner on the way to Rome. Of course I wanted to see the dungeon where he was kept prisoner. I stepped down into it, damp, dark and smelly. There was a slit of a window to the right, where a narrow beam of sunlight came through, to a fallen pillar on the dirt floor. I walked across to the pillar and sat down on it. I just sat there, watching the dust particles dance in the sunbeam.

I thought: *Is this like the way that Paul heard from heaven? To write his epistles to the Churches with such in-depth knowledge of God, to form part of our Bible today?* Not even those thick dungeon walls could stop the living waters from flowing through his life.

If any man thirst, let him come unto me, and drink. He that believeth on me, as the Scripture hath said, out of his belly shall flow rivers of living water. John 7:37-38

I thought on: *And not just one river, but many rivers, and nobody can stop a river. A river will soon pour round the banks, or even break through a dam. What are the rivers in our lives? A ministry can be a river, and a river can have different streams, like book-writing, another possibly sharing the Gospel. Another river may be a church ministry, or helps ministry or intercession, and many other rivers of service.*

"Lord, there is not even one tiny drop of water coming through my life – please, Lord, can you change me? I want rivers of living water to pour out of my life for you."

I know God heard that prayer. He has worked in my life ever since. There were plenty of obstacles obstructing His living waters (the waters of His love). These living rivers flow from Heaven into us and out through us via our ministry to others. These living waters can become blocked or obstructed in some way. One such obstacle for me was that I was extremely shy, had low self-esteem, and a fear of rejection. How could God use such a person? But guess what, God has healed me, changed me, and now uses me in an international ministry. If he can do that for me, He can do it for anybody.

Back to the present. I asked the Lord, "Lord, how do I counsel people in groups? Churches, conferences, sometimes hundreds of people at a time?" He said, "Pray with them. Ask them to take Me by the hand and take Me with them down the tunnel into their past, possibly right back into their mother's womb. On the way down the tunnel into their memory, they will see where the different hurts, problems and obstacles came into their lives. They are to imagine them as posters stuck up on the side of the tunnel of their memories. They must show them to me and allow me to remove the posters and give them a hug of love. There may only be one poster, or many. They need to do the same with each one, that I may heal them and set them free."

Let's pray and do this now.

After this, lead Jesus down the tunnel of your memory to the next poster and the next, until every negative poster in your life has been dealt with and healed by Jesus. You will then be able to walk in a new freedom in Him, free from these stings from the past with a memory that is now free from any hurt. Now Jesus will be able to flow rivers of living water through your life that will reach out to others, bringing them into freedom also.

I have preached this inner healing message the Lord gave me many times since then, often leading into praying for people's physical sicknesses as well, many of whom would receive their healing. After this the Lord led me into yet another level, where He would send down His manifest presence on the people, causing them to fall on their faces, often weeping.

This caused me to further question these rivers of living water. This Scripture speaks of the *many* rivers that should be flowing out from our lives. Was healing one river? His power another river? Yet another river being His manifest presence? It appears to me that the river of *His presence* comes in His manifest glory, because when He comes His river comes with Him. These times, of the Lord manifesting His glory amongst us, are very special and can last hours as no one wants to leave.

The next question was when does one pray for the sick? when God's manifest presence comes down? The Lord seemed to say, *"My child, do not go into healing until I complete bringing my people deeper into My presence. You need to put My presence first and wait for My instructions to pray for the sick. The healing anointing is with you always, but My manifest presence is special. There will be times that I do not want you to pray for the sick until after the meeting is over."*

This helped me to understand that His manifest presence was different to His healing anointing and covered both inner healing and physical healing.

Let's now look at what the Scriptures say about affliction (pain, distress).

This is what Jesus also died on the cross for. Jesus endured whipping for us because of His great love. Jesus endured all manner of rejection, ridicule and all else because of His great love and then He endured the cross because of His great love. Let's start with Isaiah 53.

He was despised of men and acquainted with grief: and we hid as it were our faces from Him: he was despised, and we esteemed Him not. Surely He hath born our griefs, and carried our sorrows: yet we did esteem Him stricken, smitten of God and afflicted. Isaiah 53:3-4

These verses tell us something of what Jesus was to go through and why He was to do it. They clearly state that He endured all this for us. It is **His love** for us that motivated Jesus to suffer in these ways for us.

Verse 5: "But He was wounded for our transgressions, He was bruised for our iniquities: the chastisement of our peace was upon Him and with His stripes we are healed."

This speaks of being wounded and bruised. This is physical suffering, suffering that He endured through His great love for us, that we – you and I – could be healed.

What does this say to us? How can we really understand what this is saying? How can suffering bring healing? It is highly unpleasant to suffer – why must we suffer?

There is something deeper here. First, we know that suffering and sickness is one of the curses of the fall of man, that gave the devil an opening to bring sin, sickness and death into this world. So if the kingdom of darkness brought these three curses into this world, and Jesus brought the Kingdom of Heaven into this world through His death on the cross, then we have the first clue. Jesus was the forerunner to conquering sin, sickness and death. How can I say forerunner? Was not Jesus Christ the only one to conquer sin, sickness and death? Yes, but He wants us to do so as well. *How?*

There is only one way. It's through His incredible love. **Love** is everything and the only thing we need to get victory over every inner pain (conflict) within us.

"Lord," I asked, "please, I don't want to suffer, if possible, any of this just to write this book." I was suddenly reminded of the two occasions when I arrived back from Africa very sick, once with malaria and a second time with typhoid. Was I angry about it? No. Did it stop me from travelling abroad? No. Why? It is because I saw God's work as more important than getting ill. Why?

I remembered my call from God, when He showed me one tiny drop of His *immense love* mixed with the most terrible sorrow for the people of this earth, and I burst into tears, because I could not bear it. This feeling of love and sorrow mixed is the foundation of the ministry God then gave me. It spurs me on to share His Gospel message with as many as I can. God's enormous love cannot allow me to stop or give up because I get sick. His love alone enables me to go to any country He sends me to and to endure any sufferings that go with it. His love is greater than the heat or humidity or sickness I may pick up from that country. I do have His victory at least in that area, but there is much more to learn from Him.

Yes! Life is more complicated than my little testimony.

What about you, reading this book right now?

I have no idea what you have been through, or what you are going through right now. But God does, and He is with you right now, as you call on His glorious Name.

Only He can pour out His love so fully in your life that He will bring you to victory.

It is the victory in understanding His amazing love that brings you above each pain and suffering to such a level in Him that you actually conquer the problems you are facing.

I agree with you that it is not easy, but do not give up.

Persevere in Christ, in His love, until the victory is yours.

Yet it pleased the Lord to bruise Him: he hath put Him to grief: when thou shalt make His soul an offering for sin, He shall see His seed, He shall prolong His days, and the pleasure of the Lord shall prosper in His hand. He shall see the travail of His soul and be satisfied: by His knowledge shall my righteous servant justify many: for He shall bear their iniquities. Isaiah 53:10-11

Jesus, through His glorious love, endured all this for you (and me) and for many more people worldwide. He is at hand for you right now as you call unto Him in prayer. He is nearer to you than you think. He is actually only a breath away. He is waiting for you. He wants to bring His victory into your life. He loves you so much.

Knowing that Christ, being raised from the dead, dieth no more: death hath no more dominion over Him. For in that He died, He died unto sin once: but in that He liveth

> *He liveth unto God. Likewise reckon ye also yourselves to be dead unto sin, but alive unto God through Jesus Christ our Lord.* Romans 6:9-11

Jesus has conquered sin, sickness and death, because Jesus has risen from the dead. Jesus has the victory over every weapon the devil has ever tried to attack us with. Our victory over it all is in Jesus and Him alone. He forgives our sin, He heals our sick bodies, He sets us free from the attacks of the devil, and He alone gives us eternal life.

To get this glorious victory in Christ is greater than all we may have gone through (or are going through now) to find it. It is my prayer that you may find your victory above whatever you have gone through, in His amazing and heavenly love for you.

> *Wherefore also we pray always for you, that our God would count you worthy of His calling, and fulfil all the good pleasure of His goodness and the work of faith and power. That the name of our Lord Jesus Christ may be glorified in you, and ye in Him, according to the grace of our God and the Lord Jesus Christ.* 2 Thessalonians 1:11-12

THINK

How do I throw off my limitations from the past?
What is the one key word that gets you through affliction?
Do you want God's LIVING water to flow through your life?
How do I know I can truly get the victory in Christ?
How does Isaiah 53 relate to me?
How do I receive my victory and live this victory in my everyday life?

Time to reflect/prayer

Rivers of living water can flow from heaven into you and through you.
Dwell on this. This is a promise from God's Word. Ask the Lord for these rivers to flow through you.
Seek the Lord to see if there are any blockages in you. Remember that His deep love for you conquers all.

Healed!

CHAPTER EIGHT

LIVING FROM GOD IN OUTER AFFLICTION

Rejoicing in hope; patient in tribulation; continuing instant in prayer. Romans 12:12

This verse is talking about affliction, trials, injustices and tribulations from outside of ourselves. Sometimes these are situations that we have no control over, things that we can do nothing about. We must be persistent in our prayers ("instant" here in Romans 12:12 in the Greek means to persist in a siege, as in a military operation/spiritual warfare).

These afflictions (hurts) can cause extreme anxiety, distress and inner trauma within us, causing us to worry and seek a way out. These things can also cause loss of confidence and even depression and sickness.

There are different Greek words that describe the different types of affliction. We will look at just three of them.

THLIPSIS – Confinement and pressure with no escape. This word refers to severe hardship, the pressure of being underneath a great weight. We may have heard this called "oppression".

PATHEMA – The capacity to feel strong emotion as in a deep pain, suffering, deep emotion, agony, or people suffering persecution, e.g. Exodus 2:11, *"One day after Moses had grown up, he went to his brethren and saw their affliction."*

KAKOPATHEIA – To experience affliction that seems bad or miserable from an earthly perspective, but actually is sent by God to accomplish His greater purposes (e.g. as we read in the book of Job).

It is how to deal with these afflictions that is important. We can allow them to pull us down, or we can rise above them in Christ, but *how* is the next question.

Blessed be God, even the Father of our Lord Jesus Christ, the Father of mercies, and of God of all comforts; who comforts us in all our tribulation, that we may be able to comfort them which are in any trouble, by the comfort wherewith we ourselves are comforted of God. For as the sufferings of Christ abound in us, so our consolation also aboundeth by Christ. And whether we be afflicted, it is for your consolation and salvation, which is effectual in the enduring of the same sufferings which we also suffer: or whether we be comforted, it is for your consolidation and salvation. And our hope of you is steadfast, knowing, that as ye are partakers of the sufferings, so shall ye be also of the consolation. 2 Corinthians 1:3-7

Who comforteth us in all our tribulation, that we may be able to comfort them which are in any trouble, by the comfort wherewith we ourselves are comforted of God. 1 Corinthians 1:4

Therefore brethren, we were comforted over you in all our affliction and distress by your faith. 1 Thessalonians 3:7

These Scriptures tell us that our victory comes from God, who comforts us, and that is achieved through our faith, so that we can also comfort others. But there is still more to know. The Scriptures teach us to also deal with affliction with joy. How do we attain that? Let's read more from the Scriptures. The apostle Paul said these words to the church in Corinth:

*Great is my boldness of speech towards you, great is my glorying of you: I am filled with comfort, **I am exceedingly joyful in all our tribulation.*** 2 Corinthians 7:4 (emphasis added)

This Scripture adds another dimension. Exceedingly joyful in all tribulation?

And ye became followers of us, and of the Lord, having received the word in much affliction, with joy of the Holy Ghost. 1 Thessalonians 1:6

This Scripture adds to it the great value of following God, far greater than any affliction or persecution we may need to endure to come to God for His answers.

Where does affliction or persecution come from? The kingdom of darkness, of course. When we understand that, it helps us to deal with our affliction – knowing that it is not always the person who has hurt you, but it is that evil spirit working against you.

For we wrestle not against flesh and blood, but against principalities, against power, against the rulers of the darkness of this world, against spiritual wickedness in high places. Ephesians 6:12

We are in a fight against these things and our only victory is in Christ. We need to rise up in prayer, for our victory is in

Him alone. Whatever you are going through, bring it to the Lord in prayer (leave it at the feet of Jesus and don't take it back); He is far more able to deal with it. He alone can help you, comfort you, give you His solution and fill you with His supernatural joy and peace.

> *Take my yoke upon you, and learn of me; for I am meek and lowly in heart: and ye shall find rest unto your souls.* Matthew 11:29

> *The thief cometh not, but to steal, and to kill, and to destroy: I am come that they might have life, and that they might have it more abundantly.* John 10:10

This clarifies our situations even more. Whatever is coming against us, if we come to Christ with our problem, He will change our attitude towards the problem. He will change our perspective. He will comfort and strengthen us. He will give us the strategies to rise up above the problems and to solve them.

We are also not alone in our tribulation, affliction or suffering. Many others before us have suffered the same as we may be coming through and endured it with patience.

> *Take my brethren, the prophets, who have spoken in the name of the Lord, for an example of suffering affliction, and of patience. Behold, we count them happy which endure. Ye have heard of the patience of Job, and have seen the end of the Lord; that the Lord is very pitiful, and of tender mercy.* James 5:10-11

The great men before us conquered their affliction and distress with patience and with joy. Nothing could take their joy in the Lord away. These Scriptures bring us to a totally different and higher level of dealing with our problems compared to the earthly way. God deals with things from the heavenly realm; the world deals with problems from the earthly realm. This means that God gives us a totally different place to see our problems from. We need to change our location from the worldly view to God's view on the situation we are going through, and this is done through prayer. This will bring the victory and we are not alone in discovering this.

> *...Save that the Holy Ghost witnesseth in every city, saying that bonds and afflictions abide me. But none of these things move me, neither count I my life dear unto myself, so that I might finish my course with joy, and the ministry, which I have received of the Lord Jesus, to testify the gospel of the grace of God.* Acts 20:23-24

Affliction or persecution did not touch Paul, because he lived **above these things** in the joy of the Lord. He had the right view of them. He saw them from the heavenly perspective, not the worldly perspective. If we look at problems from the worldly perspective, we will find ourselves in a horrible struggle, but if we rise up in prayer and see them from the Lord's perspective, we will become free as we rise above them (in Christ).

I struggled with an outer affliction (brought against me by an external source) which lasted for ten months. I was up and down in the way I dealt with it, until I went to the Lord and the Scriptures to find out how to rise above it. Going to the Scriptures gave me direction, but I could not understand how joy, came into it. Not until I discovered, in my case, that joy is connected with faith, the area from which we deal with the issues. Are we dealing with conflict from the earthly realm or the heavenly realm? I discovered that this is yet another blessing we receive, when we learn to **dwell** in Christ and to truly live from His presence and love and put all our trust in Him.

I also discovered that the Lord used my affliction to teach me His greater purpose. Not only has He taught me how to come to victory in my affliction both in understanding the theory and then in practice, but how to also help others in their afflictions too.

Blessed are ye, when men shall revile you, and persecute you, and say all manner of evil against you falsely, for my sake. Rejoice and be exceeding glad, for great is your reward in heaven: for so persecuted they the prophets which were before you. Matthew 5:11-12

How will we endure? We are in a similar situation today as the disciples were. Similarly we will need to endure affliction and persecution like they did, in anticipation of the soon great return of Jesus.

What is this saying to your situation? How do you experience this victory? Sometimes a friend will be able to help you and pray with you. Maybe you are all alone, or you are dealing with more than one affliction and you have no-one to confide in. If you cannot yet live from God's love, you must at least **know** His love. Maybe it's to **return to your first love**. Coming to Christ is the only way to come into victory. Pray until something happens. God will definitely help you. He will definitely answer you. He will give you the victory you need.

And they agreed: and when they had called the apostles, and beaten them, they commanded that they should not speak in the name of Jesus and let them go. And they departed from the presence of the council, rejoicing that they were counted worthy to suffer shame for His Name. Acts 5:40-41

What makes this big difference?

And (God) hath raised us up together, and made us sit together in heavenly places in Christ Jesus, that in the ages to come He might shew the exceeding riches of His grace in His kindness towards us through Christ Jesus. Ephesians 2:6-7

That is what makes the difference. Rising up in prayer, dwelling in the heavenly places in Christ Jesus and dwelling (living) In Him and **from His presence** like the disciples did. Living in Christ, and from His love and presence, makes all the difference, and enables us to rise above every negative thing into the higher level of victory over our problems in Christ.

Nay, in all these things we are more than conquerors through Him that loved us. Romans 8:37

It is in Christ that we become conquerors over every negative thing that the enemy (the devil) can throw at us. Once we have conquered every negative thing in the Spirit, we find that we have also conquered every negative thing in the physical realm and the victory becomes ours. We can then rather rejoice in our struggles, in Christ Jesus.

This week while writing this book I saw another victory over negative forces. While speaking on radio to a African country on Sunday, I was told that the people who practiced corruption were going to the courts to come against the new president who was trying to pull the country out of corruption on Tuesday. The Lord led me to say we needed to have a prayer meeting over the radio along with the plus/minus four million listeners. Suddenly the manager came in to give us 7am on Monday morning to have the radio prayer meeting.

We had a glorious Monday morning prayer meeting over radio and felt, during the last part, God's victory in the spiritual realm, that meant we would also have victory in the physical realm. As we thanked the Lord for His victory in advance, the manager came in again to say we could have a praise and thanksgiving radio service on Wednesday at 7am.

This morning, Wednesday, we truly praised and thanked the Lord for the victory He won for us yesterday. Every negative thing we bound down in the spiritual realm over radio was conquered in the physical realm and the victory was secured. The people rejoiced.

So it is with great joy and excitement that I share this wonderful truth with you and pray that you will attain a similar victory over your struggles as well, in Christ, as I have.

THINK

How do I handle affliction and tribulation?
How can I be patient in affliction and tribulation?
How can I attain joy while I handle these problems?
How does the viewpoint of seeing problems from the heavenly realm rather than the earthly realm help me?
How do I get this victory in my own personal life?

Time to reflect/prayer
There is much to reflect on in this chapter as every one of us will go through things that are out of our control. If you are going through something or someone has hurt you, or you have taken offense, you may need to forgive someone – take it to the Lord in prayer. Choose to lay it down, knowing how much He loves you and wants to heal you.

CHAPTER NINE

LIVING FROM GOD IN THE PRACTICAL

Living out of God's love in our everyday lives and practical situations is something we should all be doing. Hopefully this book will encourage you to do so, if you are not yet living from His love.

The Gospels show us how Jesus lived, and we have many wonderful practical examples of living from God's love. Reading the Gospels will certainly encourage you greatly.

About forty-five years ago, a certain person running another riding school was spreading untrue rumours about me in order to get some of my clients. I did not know how to handle this problem, so I took it to the Lord. The Lord encouraged me to read in the Gospels of how Jesus reacted to handling untrue accusations against Him. After reading the four Gospels right through to study how Jesus reacted, I discovered that Jesus actually handled every accusation against Him with love.

Every time I had a problem, I would read through the four Gospels to see how Jesus dealt with the situation. I decided to respond in exactly the same way as Jesus did. It was life-changing. Instead of losing out, as I thought would happen, the people who had caused my problem were no longer my enemies – they actually became my friends! The Lord then asked me to forgive this person who had hurt me and to give her my first book that He had given me to write. I did not want to do this, but reluctantly obeyed. She not only received the book graciously, but actually read the book and responded to it. She phoned me to thank me for the book and told me she had received Jesus as her Lord and Saviour. We have been friends ever since.

I have always tried to react to each situation as Jesus would and it has always worked out. Jesus shows us in Scripture that by living from God's presence we have greater understanding, wisdom and knowledge in both day-to-day situations and in business situations.

Practical wisdom

...Wherein He hath abounded toward us in all wisdom and prudence. Having made known unto us the mystery of His will, according to His good pleasure which He has purposed to Himself, that in the fullness of times He might gather together in one all things in Christ, both which are in heaven, and which are on earth: even in Him. Ephesians 1:8-10

Jesus gives us His insights to make intelligent decisions by following His life applications (in the will of God) operating through our lives as we obey Him.

In active, practical ways

...Even as the Son of man came, not to be ministered unto, but to minister, and to give His life a ransom for many. Matthew 20:28

As Jesus came and ministered in so many practical ways for us, so we ought to also minister to others in a practical way. Even as Jesus walked this earth, He preached the message and began to minister to them.

And many women were there beholding from afar off, which followed Jesus from Galilee, ministering unto Him. Matthew 27:55

I believe they prepared food for Him in a practical way.

In practical knowledge

If thou put the brethren in remembrance of these things, thou shalt be a good minister of Jesus Christ, nourished up in the words of faith and of good doctrine, whereunto thou hast attained. 1 Timothy 4:6

Studying the Word of God will nourish us and build us up in our faith, so that it is easier to serve the Lord, having both heard Him and gained the knowledge as to what Scripture teaches us. Faith can then be worked out through our lives.

And He touched her hand and the fever left. Matthew 8:15

In the same way, this knowledge that Jesus wants to heal the sick gives us the faith to obey the Lord and do similar things. *As we obey Him,* so He does the miraculous healing through our hands.

In the practical business of everyday life

We need to accomplish what is necessary in a practical and reliable way. Every type of work that we do always has incalculable eternal worth, when our work is done in faith, obeying God, in His worked persuasions within us.

Now Faith is the substance of things hoped for, the evidence of things not seen. Hebrews 11:1

The whole chapter (Hebrews 11) speaks on faith – please read it.

When the Lord told us to build a 50-bed residential holiday facility for church camps, etc., without money, without borrowing, without a mortgage, it took a bit of faith. We were then offered £50,000 from the Lottery fund to build it. But we would have to have their logo on our website and so on. I prayed about it and the Lord said, "Do you want me to provide, or man to provide?" "You, Lord," I replied and turned down the offer.

The Lord did provide, even down to matching sheets and pillowcases, all from our mere £8.50 and prayer. I praise the Lord for what He has done at Standlake Equestrian Centre and Ranch. That is our God.

THINK

Why should we take everything to God in prayer?
Why is it a good idea to look up how Jesus reacted to certain situations?
In what practical ways should we respond to God?
How can we serve God in our everyday life?

Time to reflect/prayer

Ask the Lord if there is anything that He wants you to do for Him. Remember, "Nothing is impossible with God."

CHAPTER TEN

LIVING FROM GOD'S LOVE

That they all may be one, as thou, Father, art in me, and I in Thee, that they may also be one in us: that the world may believe that thou hast sent me. John 17:21

I in them, and thou in me, that they may be made perfect in one: and that the world may know that thou hast sent me, and thou hast loved them as thou hast loved me. John 17:23

This is part of the great prayer Jesus prayed before going to the cross.

Everything that Jesus had done on earth was motivated out of love. Every teaching He gave us was motivated out of love; every healing, every deliverance, everyone He raised from the dead was motivated by His compassion and love. Now He was praying for you and me to also be motivated by love.

We can only be motivated from His love if we live in Him and He in us. It is only as we also live from God's love that **the world will see** that we are His disciples.

This is why prayer is so important. Without contact with the Lord in prayer, it is impossible for us to live from His love and presence, or love others as we should. Only in Him will living from His love become possible. Only as we live from God's love will the world see and know that He has sent us, that Jesus is truly alive, that the Bible is true and trustworthy. It is then that people will respond to Jesus for their own lives.

In 1980 in Israel, we were not allowed to share our faith with others, but we were allowed to live it. We were also allowed to answer questions that others asked in an open and truthful way.

I was there for a gap year working on Kibbutz Einat, near Tel Aviv. I was working in the kitchen and dining room at the time and had recently been baptised, fully emerged, in the river Jordan. I was excited in the Lord and was learning from Him daily. I just wanted to tell everyone about Jesus, yet was not allowed to. "Lord," I asked, "how do I share the Gospel message in these conditions?"

"Just live it," came the reply.

I then worked to the best of my ability. When the bell sounded for us to finish work, everyone working in the kitchen would suddenly vanish. I looked around me and went ahead to complete any unfinished jobs and then I would leave myself. After a week or two of completing the work and leaving the kitchen later, an elderly gentleman who used to stay in the dining room to read his newspaper after lunch called me over. "I have been watching you," he said, "and I want to ask you a question. Why do you stay on to finish the work in the kitchen after the others have left?" "Because it needs doing," I replied. "No, it's more than that," he went on. "Well, I suppose I am trying to live out my Christian faith." "Now that makes a better reason," he told me, "I want to ask you some questions on your Christian faith. Would you be happy to come and sit down opposite me so I can ask these questions?" "Sure," I replied and sat down.

Every day after that, I went over to him and he asked many questions, some of them so difficult, that I had to do some research on them, so I spent the rest of the day doing just that. One day, I felt led to give him a book on poetry that I had written, and he received it gladly. The next day he called me over again to say that he had received the One whom the book spoke of as his true Lord.

I later discovered that this man was a retired rabbi, and he kept in contact with me for a couple more years for encouragement, as he was now a secret believer. This experience I can never forget. It is living our faith, out of God's love, that speaks far more powerfully than words. It is living out our faith in the practical, hopefully from His love, that speaks volumes.

What type of love was I doing all this from? was one of the difficult questions that I needed to research for the old man, and I discovered that there are different types of love explained in the Greek language. After all, I definitely did not have any affection for that sprawling kibbutz kitchen, nor for the old man, so what was motivating me to do all this research?

I discovered that there are a few Greek words for love: *Eros* (sexual love), *Storge* (parental love), *Phileo* (brotherly affection/loving friend). But the love we will look into is another Greek word for love, and that is AGAPE love. *Agape* is the highest form of love (the Old Testament speaks also of CHARITY) – as in the love of God for mankind. A love that originates in God, a self-sacrificial love.

Agape can speak of an abounding love for many. So I looked at these Scriptures.

> *By this shall all men know that ye are my disciples, if you have love one to another.* John 13:35

Straightforward enough, but I needed more explanation.

> *As the Father hath loved me, so have I loved you: continue ye in my love.* John 15:9

This is my commandment, that ye love one another, as I have loved you. Greater love hath no man than this, that a man lay down his life for his friends. John 15:12-13

Jesus laid down His life on the cross out of His Love for us. In the last verse of His great prayer, before He went to the cross, He prayed:

And I have declared unto them thy Name, and will declare it: that the love wherewith thou has loved me may be in them, and I in them. John 17:26

This says it all! We have no love like this within us, unless we receive it from God, and have Jesus living within us. We need both the love of God within us and Jesus living in our hearts. Only then can we live from God's love.

How can this happen?

And hope maketh not ashamed; because the love of God is shed abroad in our hearts by the Holy Ghost which is given to us. Romans 5:5

We have to be born again, we have to be baptised in the Holy Spirit. Then, through the Holy Spirit, we can receive God's great love within us, from which nothing can separate us.

Who shall separate us from the love of Christ? Shall tribulation, or distress, or persecution, or famine, or nakedness, or peril, or sword? Romans 8:35

Nay, in all these things we are more than conquerors through Him that loved us. For I am persuaded that neither death, nor life, nor angels, nor principalities, nor powers, nor things present, nor things to come, nor height, nor depth, nor any other creature, shall be able to separate us from the love of God, which is in Christ Jesus our Lord. Romans 8:37-39

The above Scripture says it all! How great God's love is, and how amazing that we can receive His love through the Holy Spirit, given to us from Jesus.

The next question to answer was: **What else can we do to receive His great love?**

Let love be without dissimulation. Abhor that which is evil, cleave to that which is good. Romans 12:9

Love worketh no ill to his neighbour: therefore love is the fulfilment of the law. Romans 13:10

Love in the old King James Version also speaks of *Agape* love using the word "charity".

Charity suffereth long, and is kind: Charity envieth not: Charity vaunteth not itself, is not puffed up, doth not behave itself unseemly, seeketh not her own, is not easily provoked, thinketh no evil: Rejoiceth not in iniquity, but rejoiceth in the truth; Beareth all things, believeth all things, hopeth all things, endureth all things. Charity never faileth: but where there be prophecies, they shall fail; whether there be tongues, they shall cease; whether there be knowledge, it shall vanish away. For we know in part, and we prophecy in part. But when that which is perfect is come, then that which is in part shall be done away. 1 Corinthians 13:4-10 KJV

What would be the result? To live in righteousness In Him, In His Love.

Beloved, let us love one another: for love is of God: and every one that loveth is born of God and knoweth God. He that loveth not knoweth not God; for God is Love. In this was manifested the love of God toward us, because that God sent His only begotten Son into the world, that we might live through Him. Herein is love, not that we loved God, but that He loved us, and sent His Son to be the propitiation for our sins. Beloved, If God so loved us, we ought also to love one another. No man hath seen God at any time. If we love one another, God dwelleth in us, and His love is perfected in us. 1 John 4:7-12

And we have known and believed the love that God hath to us. God is Love: and he that dwelleth in love dwelleth in God, and God in him. 1 John 4:16

Sharing these Scriptures with the elderly man in the kibbutz dining room not only brought him to Christ, but taught and prepared me for the ministry ahead, that the Lord had prepared for me.

I pray that these Scriptures will also encourage you to seek God and live out of His love in this needy world that we live in.

THINK

Living out our faith speaks far more than words: explain.
What else can we do, apart from receiving His love?
Explain 1 John 4:16.
What is the love of God?

Time to reflect/prayer

You may want to read this chapter over again and again. Walking in the love of God (this Agape *love) can only come from the Lord.*
Reflect on your walk. Are you walking in righteousness and love? Ask the Lord to reveal to you why this chapter is so important.

Standlake Conference Guests

CHAPTER ELEVEN

LIVING FROM GOD'S REST

Rest comes from the Greek word *Katapausis*. Rest speaks of intermission from labour, refreshment, to lie down and rest, to be refreshed in one's spirit. It also speaks of peace and quietness, of a loosening, relaxation, relief, freedom, to be silent.

For If Jesus had given them rest, He would not afterward have spoken of another day. There remaineth therefore a rest to the people of God. For he that is entered into his rest, he also hath ceased from his own works, as God did from His. Let us labour therefore to enter into that rest, lest any man fall after the same example of unbelief. Hebrews 4:8-12

This strong passage comes with a warning for some of us who get so caught up in work that we backslide as a result. We start working in the flesh rather than in the Spirit, from God's love. God is trying to teach us that the better way is through **resting** in Him, so that we can hear His still small voice, that carries great power, to then live in obedience from His love.

For He spake in a certain place of the seventh day on this wise: And God did rest on the seventh day from all His works. And in this place again: If they shall enter into my rest. Hebrews 4:4-5

Remember the Word which Moses the servant of the Lord commanded you, saying, "The Lord your God hath given you rest, and hath given you this land." Joshua 1:13

Therefore he said unto Judah, "Let us build these cities, and make about them walls, and towers, gates, and bars, while the land is yet before us; because we have sought the Lord our God, we have sought Him, and He hath given us rest on every side." So they built and prospered. 2 Chronicles 14:7

Studying these verses reveals both practical and spiritual results when we enter **His rest.** It is only in resting in God that we are quiet enough to hear Him and then obey Him. If we have heard Him, then we will have the faith to obey Him. If we obey Him, we can also **rest in Him.** Even in adverse situations, resting in Him shall guide your way.

After Paul had asked the Lord three times to remove the thorn from his flesh, he wrote:

Therefore I take pleasure in infirmities, in reproaches, in necessities, in persecutions, in distresses for Christ's sake: for when I am weak, then I am strong. 2 Corinthians 12:10

This is the result of truly resting in Him. Truly we can say, when we are weak, He is strong. In our weakness, we allow God to work through our lives, rather than us trying to do it in our own strength (striving to do it).

His strength is so much greater than our strength. His way of doing things is so much more efficient and effective than our ways of doing things. When we realise how important it is that God has His way in us, we will never again neglect entering into His glorious rest, and learning to live from His great love.

It is our God, our Lord and Saviour who does it all. All we need to do is yield to Him and enter His presence, rest in His presence, live in His presence and then live *from* His presence (heavenly realm) and His love. It is possible to do this in the world we live in despite what we are going through.

THINK

What does rest speak of?
Why should we keep a Sabbath day?
Why should we labour to enter His rest?
What are the results of resting in Christ?

Take time to reflect/prayer

Our deepest desire should be to REST in God and to remain in His REST and to live out of His REST. Ask the Lord to help you to do this. It is good to meditate on Scriptures on REST as I did, and as you study, I feel sure the Lord will give you fresh revelation and speak to you.

CONCLUSION

We need to move more and more into His glorious presence. We need to thank Him daily and praise Him without ceasing. We need to worship Him daily and allow Him to change us more into His likeness. The world is more impressed by our "walk" than our "talk".

I have shared with you my personal testimony of what the Lord has been teaching and changing in me over many years. Very few believers are prepared to share with others what their personal relationship with the Lord is really like. Some are unaware that it is possible to have an intimate relationship with God and would even insist that this is not possible. My prayer is that, as you read this book over and over again, the Lord will pour His love into your heart and use you for His glory.

Every chapter in this book is a progression. Practice Chapter 1 before you move to Chapter 2, and so on. We are all on a journey with God. When you feel confident in going through the Tabernacle and entering His presence, then move on to practicing hearing the Lord's voice and obeying Him.

At the end of this book, there is a personal testimony from Joy Johnson. After hearing some of this teaching she had a hunger for more and decided to do her own research, and she "found" this intimacy in God.

This book is for you if you are hungering for more of God, and if you have a deep desire to hear His voice and know your calling.

Everything a believer does should be rooted in God's love, and this comes from our time spent in prayer, in His presence, and living a righteous life is just as important.

It may take you some time to grasp fully each chapter, but don't worry, the main thing to remember is that the more *we draw close to Him, He draws close to us.* Persevere – don't give up.

On the chapter on abiding and dwelling in Him, my question to you is: Who wouldn't want to dwell with the One they love?

As I was discussing this book with a friend, I discovered that their prayer was for "rivers of living water" to flow from within them through to others. We both had similar revelations that these waters come from the Throne Room of God into us. These rivers are alive (they truly are "living" waters) because they are rivers of HIS LOVE! You can ask the Lord for the same revelation as you spend time in His presence.

I speak of living a life of righteousness and can't express how important this is. Our "fruit" is of far more importance to God than our "gifts". The Holy Spirit is the giver of gifts, but we (as part of our yielding ourselves to Him) are responsible for the fruit of the Holy Spirit (Galatians 5).

I say in this book that "we must hear God" – if we don't hear His voice, we can't obey Him. Some of you may never have heard God speak to you. My prayer is that this will become a reality for you.

Everyone at some time will go through affliction, whether it is physical or spiritual. It is dealing with this from the heavenly realm that I have learned over time; that works for me. It's all about doing what Jesus did. Walk as He walked. Depend on the Father and spend time with the Father. As the Father speaks, obey Him and allow God to move through you in a very powerful way.

As I have shared these truths with you, my prayer is that you will discover the love that the Lord has for you. Know that there is an intimacy that comes from abiding in Him, and we can DWELL in Him! I pray that as you hear God's voice, He will lead you into that ministry that He has already planned for you, and many rivers of His living water will be poured into you and through you.

Please do not just read the words in this book; seek God seriously that you may experience in depth His liquid love and life-changing power. Not a second seeking Him could ever be wasted, but rewarded instead in this life and for all eternity by His everlasting love.

If you would like to contact me, my email is suzannesministries@gmail.com

My husband and I believe it's the Lord's vision for us to set up a beautiful retreat. This would be for families, pastors or individuals to come and spend a few days to seek the Lord, ask questions and get prayer for personal situations or healing. This could possibly happen this year, 2019. Get in touch for details. Meanwhile we will carry on holding the popular teaching and healing weekends at Standlake Ranch in Oxfordshire, UK. Phone +44 (0)1865 300099 for prayer over the phone or to book your weekend with us.

You are also welcome to do our discipleship training course free of charge on our website or watch our many teaching broadcasts on YouTube; just type in Suzanne Pillans for YouTube, or our website is suzannesministries.co.uk which will also lead you to our YouTube videos.

TESTIMONY TIME

And they overcame him by the blood of the Lamb, and by the word of their testimony; and they loved not their lives unto the death. Revelation 12:11

Joy Johnson: Testimony (Going Through the Tabernacle)

My journey into the presence of God becoming a reality in my life began with Suzanne's preaching on this topic and then reading her book *Dare to Enter His Presence*. One reading was not sufficient, but over a period of two years I read this book four times, each time learning and understanding more.

I came to realise that there was another level of prayer and seeking God and His presence that I knew nothing about, even though I had been a Christian for 49 years, and I was hungry to experience this.

When Suzanne visited New Zealand in March 2017 she preached on the Tabernacle and how it was laid out, and how by using this pattern, we can enter God's presence. My desire was to learn and experience more.

In one of Suzanne's meetings in 2017, people from many different nations were there and Suzanne taught on the Tabernacle and led us through the various stages until we entered into the Holy of Holies. Then it happened: the Lord's presence so filled the room that I hardly dared to breathe. The presence was so holy that I kept my eyes shut, not moving a muscle; there was a perfectly holy fear in His presence. It lasted for a long time. No one could move. There were people crying and everyone was experiencing the Lord's presence.

This encounter made me so hungry to know God on a deeper level. It also affected Suzanne, so that subsequent arrivals of the presence of God began to happen after her preaching on the Tabernacle pattern of prayer. All through 2017 I was on a quest to read as much as I could about the Tabernacle's tent layout, how it was set up and what each item actually represented. I read and re-read the relevant Bible passages. I googled "Tabernacle" and read copious articles written about it.

I read Derek Prince's book *Entering the Presence of God*, where he had a chapter about the Tabernacle pattern of prayer, but still I did not have the revelation regarding it.

Then one day at the end of December 2017, while still searching, I found Dr David Yonggi Cho's book on "Praying the Temple Prayer" online. Finally, everything began to make sense and all the knowledge I had gained came together like a finished jigsaw puzzle.

From the beginning of 2018, every day for four months I prayed through Yonggi Cho's temple prayer. Most days it took three to four hours to go right through the ten pages. It took so long because the Holy Spirit was speaking to me about things in my life He wanted to deal with, as well as teaching me revelations from the Word of God. Our times were filled with such closeness and intimacy that the hours just seemed like minutes. In the hours I spent waiting on God and working through the prayer, I began to experience a peace and stillness within me that enveloped me through the day.

I learned how easy it is to flow in the Spirit in what I said and did, when this peace was reigning in me. I also began to learn what could disturb the peace: things I did or attitudes I held that offended the Holy Spirit. I quickly would say, "What is it, Holy Spirit, that has come between us?" and He would tell me. My task then was to repent and ask for forgiveness, and then came crying out to Him to help me overcome in that area. As I yielded to Him, it made me more and more aware of my total dependence upon Him for everything.

I am so glad we are on a journey, not having yet reached our destination, and He is still continuing to mould me into the likeness of Jesus.

To sum up, entering His presence and living in His presence requires something that is most precious to us all: our time. It also requires yielding and obedience to the Holy Spirit's leading and guidance, and a day-by-day dependence on Him. But oh, the joy of walking so close to the Lord, hearing His loving, correcting voice, living life out from the stillness and peace within. The world has absolutely nothing that can compare to it.

My prayer for everyone who reads this book of Suzanne's and reads this testimony is that you would hunger and thirst after God with all your heart, soul and mind and press into Him until you daily experience living in His presence.

May God bless you as you journey with Him.

Joy Johnson

---o--O--o---

Elizabeth Adu Gyekye: Testimony (Hearing God's Voice)
Rev. Suzanne and myself were invited to Mandapeta, India (for the Mandapeta Annual Church Convention), a suburb of one of the cities, as missionaries to preach the gospel during one of their conventions in 2015.

On the third day of the programme, Rev. Suzanne, just after preaching, was informed by the Lord to leave the tent immediately. She pulled me by the hand and we went into the house. Two minutes later a relieved host told us that 20 armed activists had arrived to arrest us, and told us to go upstairs and hide in our room.

In the night we prayed and asked the Lord God to protect us throughout the programme. This enabled us to seek the face of the Lord and ask for His presence to be with us through the power of the Holy Spirit and to drive away territorial spirits and to scatter every stronghold.

On the following day we heard a knock on the door. There was someone at the door telling us not to come out of the room, because the group of 20 activists who had come to the programme the night before had arrived again and were asking for the missionaries who had come from the UK. They wanted us to come out from hiding, but we knew we must stay there quietly till everything had calmed down.

We prayed continuously. Whilst we were praying, we heard another knock, followed by banging on the door. Suzanne whispered to keep totally silent. She was lying on her bed praying. We were so silent we hardly breathed, and after a time of banging the men left the door. Later on in the day we were called to preach as the activists had gone.

Next day we were told to stay in the room again, because the activists had returned. After that I had an encouraging vision that the Lord would protect us, as well as the salvation of two of the activists. I prayed and gave Him thanks.

This encounter really helped me with my walk with God. I also benefited greatly from the book Suzanne gave me, *Step Out in Faith*.

Whilst we were still waiting in our room, one of the pastors came to call us to come down to the convention grounds with the information that the men had disappeared, so Rev. Suzanne could preach the gospel as scheduled. She gave thanks to God and preached powerfully under the unction of the Holy Spirit.

On the last day, only ten of the activists arrived, this time unarmed. They were so impacted by the Gospel message that they wanted to know more about God. Two of the activists gave their lives to Christ and were baptised that very morning. Suzanne and I crept over to watch them getting baptised from the upstairs veranda. God knows how to turn His children to Him.

Honestly, I saw that we were in danger, hearing about twenty activists ready and waiting for us on the platform, but God delivered us. With praying and obedience we overcame the enemy. The Lord said we should fear not, for He is with us. The result of trusting in the Lord in times of trouble is powerful. When you are in danger, put your trust in the Lord.

My relationship with the Lord was built up, so my worries disappeared. They did not bother me anymore. As Christians we live for God and His love moves us to obey His voice and trust in Him, so that we will not fear when we face the storms of life.

To God be the glory for great things He did for us, the two activists gave their lives to Christ and were baptised. This is the power of God and what He can do even in the midst of a difficult situation.

Elizabeth Adu Gyekye

--o--0--o--

Nicholas Bensted M.A.(Oxon) BA (Hons) Dip (Dship&Min): Testimony

Suzanne's writings have been a great encouragement to me in the work of evangelism I do as a missionary in Thailand.

I know of her hard work, perseverance, discernment and reliance on the Holy Spirit from her ministry here, and so regularly refer to her written work as an encouragement.

PERSONAL NOTES/REFLECTIONS/GOD SPEAKING TO YOU

PERSONAL NOTES/REFLECTIONS/GOD SPEAKING TO YOU

SOME OF SUZANNE'S OTHER BOOKS

Dare to Breakthrough The Impossible with Christ

Do you dare to do great exploits for God, or be set free from sickness or bondage? God has done impossible things for Suzanne Pillans and enabled her to break through into a powerful and miraculous ministry. By the victory of His death on the Cross Christ has already overcome any difficulty life might bring on us, this book will help you to take hold of that victory – if you dare!

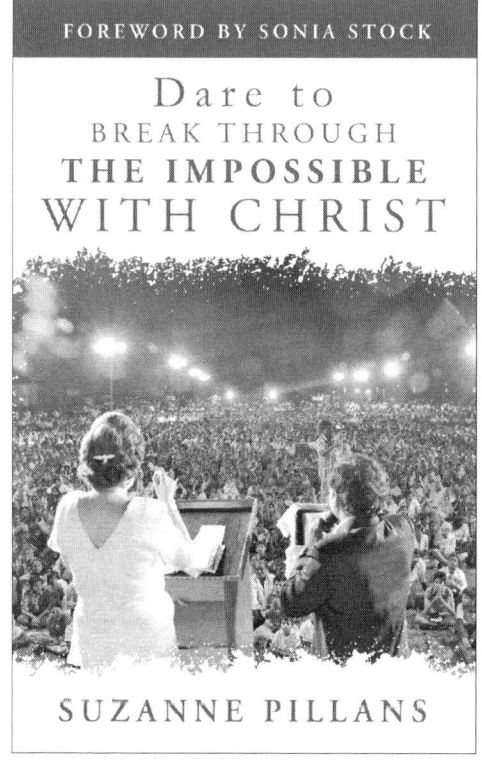

SOME OF SUZANNE'S OTHER BOOKS

Dare to Search for Truth

The amazing story of Suzanne's desperate search for the truth after her horse Jacky Boy was hit by a card
　Her search for an answer to save Jacky Boy ended up changing Suzanne's life and redirecting her to achieving more than she could ever imagine
　The book is a gripping story about the issues of life that we struggle with and discovering the answer to them.

SOME OF SUZANNE'S OTHER BOOKS

Dare to Enter His Presence

This book teaches on prayer and the glorious relationship the Lord offers each one of us to have in Him as we dare to enter His presence. 'This book is the evidence of the power and anointing which has begun to follow her ministry, firstly in the 'Fire over Kenya' Conference, then wherever she has gone in obedience to the call of God.' From the Foreword by David Hathaway, President of Eurovision.

SOME OF SUZANNE'S OTHER BOOKS

Dare to Step Out in Faith

This book will encourage you to search the Word and to pray until you are fired up to go in Christ's name. It will help you realise the importance of knowing the power that God releases when we serve Him.

Allow the words in this book to erupt within the fibres of your being and help you walk in all He created you to be.

SOME OF SUZANNE'S OTHER BOOKS

Dare to Walk in Power, Authority and Love

Teaching on the miraculous and using the Authority of the Name of Jesus. The book is written in three parts:

- the Protection of God;
- the Authority of Jesus; and
- the Love and Grace of God

The book Dares You to enter into the miracle ministry of God by simple faith and obedience to the Word of God.

SOME OF SUZANNE'S OTHER BOOKS

Dare to do ONLY the Father's Will

Suzanne writes about Living from within God's Presence. Using examples from her life she writes about two key topics:

- How to hear God clearly
- Do only what God is telling you to do

Suzanne shows in this book that God uses ordinary people to demonstrate His power and glory. The Bible says that not many high or mighty are called , but 'God has choses the weak to confound the mighty.'